How the Bible Came to Be

How the Bible Came to Be

JOHN BARTON

WESTMINSTER
JOHN KNOX PRESS
LOUISVILLE · KENTUCKY

Cover design by Jennifer K. Cox

First published in 1997 by
DLT, London

First American edition 1998
Published by Westminster John Knox Press
Louisville, Kentucky

This book is printed on acid-free paper that meets the
American National Standards Institute Z39.48 standard. ♾

PRINTED IN THE UNITED STATES OF AMERICA

08 09 — 12 11 10 9 8

Library of Congress Cataloging-in-Publication Data
is on file at the Library of Congress, Washington, D.C.

ISBN-13: 978-0-664-25785-9
ISBN-10: 0-664-25785-2

Contents

Preface

The history of the biblical canon has been an interest of mine for the last 15 years or so. Having discussed it in a technical way in two books (*Oracles of God: Perceptions of Ancient Prophecy in Israel after the Exile*, Darton, Longman and Todd 1986, and *The Spirit and the Letter: Studies in the Biblical Canon*, SPCK 1997), I am glad to have a chance in the present book to sum up my findings in a less formal way. It is not in the nature of this book to include a detailed discussion of the intricate questions which make up the problem of the canon – but it is only fair to warn the reader that much of what I say is fairly controversial, especially the way I use the word 'canon' itself. The two longer books just mentioned set out the case for what is presented here without the supporting arguments.

There are two appendices: a glossary of technical terms, and brief biographies of some early writers who have a bearing on the origin of the Christian Bible. All biblical quotations are taken from the Revised Standard Version.

I must thank my original commissioning editor, Lesley Riddle, and David Moloney, my present editor at DLT, one for launching this project and the other for seeing it through to completion many years later. Publishers need patience with authors like me.

The book is dedicated with much love to my father, Bernard Barton.

John Barton
April 1997

Introduction

'In the name of the Holy Scripture we do understand those Canonical Books of the Old and New Testaments, of whose authority was never any doubt in the Church.' In these words, Article VI of the Church of England's 39 Articles of Religion of 1563 formulated an idea that is still common today. This is the idea that what we now know as 'the Bible' has existed in exactly its present form from the earliest days of the Christian Church, unchanged and unchallenged. In our culture, the Bible is monolithic. Few people read it seriously, but everyone knows what it looks like: a single volume, printed in double columns, and always containing exactly the same books. To know the names of all those books is a rare accomplishment today, but most people would be startled to think that they might vary from one edition to another. The Bible is the Bible: it has always been the same and always will be the same, whether we like it or not.

The idea of 'Holy Scripture' seems to contain within it this implication of completeness, fixity, and stability. The books of the Bible are experienced as a given, and their authority lies in the fact that it is God who gave them: they are not in any way negotiable, and they cannot be questioned. This can no doubt be seen as a great advantage for the Christian, whose faith thus rests not on the shifting sands of human teaching but on the firm rock of a God-given revelation. Yet the result can also be that the Bible becomes rather two-dimensional – lacking the depth and variety of ordinary books. Faced with any other collection of books, we should want to know when they were written and why; how they came to be collected together, and for what purpose. With the Bible such questions tend to be suppressed. The result can be an impoverishment in our understanding. Paradoxically, the very holiness and authority of the Bible can have the effect of suppressing in our minds many of the questions we ask about other books, with the result that we find it less interesting than many books of far less religious prestige. (A partial analogy might be the way in which Shakespeare's status at the summit of English literature can get in the way of many people's enjoyment of him: he is 'a classic', hived off into a kind of ghetto of works too important to be interesting.)

In this book we shall try to break down the monolithic character of the Bible by asking simple questions about its origins. These fall into two categories, which overlap to some extent but which can be considered separately. First, how and when did the various books in the Bible come to be written? Second, how were they collected together to form the 'Scriptures' of the Old and New Testaments? In the twentieth century more attention has been paid to the first of these questions than to the second, but both are necessary if we want to understand how we got our Bible, and what kind of work it is.

It is always satisfying if the answers to one's questions turn out to be very simple – though it can be more interesting if they do not. Where the Bible is concerned, the level of interest is high, for the answers are complex, sometimes uncertain, and always rather speculative; and for some people this inevitably makes them also rather unsatisfactory. But the Bible is an enormous and complicated work, an anthology of literature from many times and places, and this makes it inherently unlikely that the story of its growth and origin will be simple and easy.

Even so, we shall have to be selective in telling this story, to avoid going endlessly down culs-de-sac. Not every book in the Bible will be described and analysed, as is done systematically in the kind of work traditionally called an 'Introduction' (in a technical sense of the word). What is offered here is a conducted tour around some of the most important questions, with selective illustrations taken from particular books. The aim is to paint with a broad brush, not to fill in all the fine detail.

CHAPTER ONE

The Contents of the Bible

This book describes how the various books of the Bible came to be written and how, in due course, they became the Scriptures of the Christian Church. Most of what is said here presupposes that the reader has a broad general knowledge of the contents of the Bible, where to find this or that book, what it is about – but not about when or how it was written. This chapter looks briefly at the contents of the Bible. Readers who already have this basic knowledge could skip this chapter – but others may find that it tells them (or reminds them of) some of the things they need to know to get the best value from the rest of this book.

THE OLD TESTAMENT

As later chapters will explain, there are two versions of the Old Testament currently in circulation: Catholic and Protestant (the Jewish Bible has the same contents as the Protestant Old Testament, but in a different order). We will follow the Catholic order, clearly indicating those books which are not found in the Protestant version.

Genesis
The history of humankind from the creation of the world to the deeds of Abraham, Isaac, Jacob, and Joseph – the 'Patriarchs'.

Exodus
The story of the Israelites in Egypt, their escape ('exodus') under the leadership of Moses, the law-giving at Mount

Sinai (including the Ten Commandments), and the setting up of the sacred tent to travel with the people on their way to the Promised Land.

Leviticus
Further detailed laws given at Sinai.

Numbers
Further laws; then the story of the departure of the Israelites from Sinai towards the borders of the Promised Land. The stories of Balak and Balaam the sorcerer.

Deuteronomy
Moses' last words to the Israelites, giving them further laws to be observed in the Promised Land; the death of Moses.

These five books are sometimes called the Pentateuch, and sometimes the Five Books of Moses.

Joshua
The account of the conquest of some of Palestine under Moses' successor, Joshua.

Judges
Further settlement in the Promised Land. Israel is ruled by a succession of 'judges' – half kings, half military commanders – such as Deborah, Gideon and Samson.

Ruth
A story, set in the time of the judges, about a Moabite woman who settles in Israel and marries a wealthy Israelite farmer.

1 Samuel
The transition from the judges to the monarchy under the guidance of Samuel: stories about Saul, Israel's first king.

2 Samuel
David succeeds Saul, who is killed in battle with the Philistines. The detailed story of how Solomon then succeeded David, with David's other children being involved in murder, rape and incest.

1 Kings
An account of the reign of Solomon, the division of the kingdom into north and south (Israel and Judah) on his death; the earliest kings of the divided kingdoms; the work of the prophet Elijah.

2 Kings
The work of the prophet Elisha. Stories of the later kings of Israel and Judah; Josiah's reform of the state religion. The invasion of Judah first by the Assyrians, then by the Babylonians; the exile of the people of Judah to Babylonia.

1 Chronicles
The history of the world down to David, much of it told through genealogical lists ('begats').

2 Chronicles
The history from Solomon to the Exile, following the story in 2 Kings but with many differences of detail, and including the restoration of Judah by the Persians at the end of the Exile.

Ezra
The story of how the Persian king sent various exiled Judaeans back to Judah to rebuild the Temple and re-establish the religion, including a priest, Ezra.

Nehemiah
An account (often in the first person) of the activities of Nehemiah, a Jew appointed as Persian governor of Judah at around the same time as Ezra.

Tobit

A story (omitted from Protestant Bibles) about pious Jews who succeed in forming a marriage alliance between branches of their family despite the opposition of kings and demons, thanks to the help of an angel.

Judith

The story (not in Protestant Bibles) of a Jewish heroine who tricked the commander of the Assyrian army and decapitated him, thereby saving Israel from defeat.

Esther

A story about a Jew, Esther, taken into the Persian king's harem, who saved her fellow Jews from a threatened pogrom. (The Catholic version is considerably longer than the Protestant, with additions at various places in the book.)

The books from Joshua to Esther (or sometimes from Genesis to Esther) are often known as the historical books.

Job

The story of a righteous man who suffers severely, tries to understand his suffering in dialogue with three friends, and is eventually restored to prosperity.

Psalms

One hundred and fifty hymns, prayers, and songs, attributed to David.

Proverbs

Wise sayings and short paragraphs of teaching about ethical and practical conduct, attributed to Solomon.

Ecclesiastes

A book of sceptical reflections on the meaning of life (or lack of it), attributed to Solomon.

The Song of Songs, or **The Song of Solomon**
A collection of love-poems.

The Wisdom of Solomon
Further teaching about human conduct and divine wisdom, attributed to Solomon. (This book is not included in Protestant Bibles.)

Sirach, or **Ecclesiasticus,** or **The Wisdom of Jesus son of Sira**
Further lengthy collection of proverbs and more extensive teaching (also absent from Protestant Bibles). Jesus ben Sira lived in the second century BC.

The books from Job to Sirach are sometimes known as the didactic or teaching books

Isaiah
Lengthy prophecies attributed to Isaiah, who lived in the eighth century BC. Chapters 40—55 are the source of many Christian images, including the 'suffering servant', and provided much of the text for Handel's *Messiah*.

Jeremiah
The longest of the prophetic books, whose core is the sayings of Jeremiah, who lived from the late seventh century BC down into the time of Exile in the sixth century BC.

Lamentations
Five solemn laments over the fall of Jerusalem to the Babylonians, traditionally attributed to Jeremiah.

Baruch
A book, not in the Protestant Bible, attributed to Jeremiah's secretary Baruch, and reflecting on the Exile in both penitence and hope. (Chapter 6 is sometimes named separately as **The Letter of Jeremiah**.)

Ezekiel
The prophecies of a younger contemporary of Jeremiah, including his visions of God enthroned above a chariot pulled by mysterious beasts, and of the dry bones which came back to life as a symbol of the rebirth of the nation after the Exile.

Daniel
Stories and visions, purportedly by a contemporary of Jeremiah, who was exiled but rose to favour in Babylon through his power to interpret dreams. The lions' den, the burning fiery furnace, and the writing on the wall are well-known episodes from Daniel.

Susannah (or Daniel 13)
A short detective story, whose hero is Daniel, in which a Jewish woman, Susannah, is saved from false accusations of adultery brought against her by two men who have been thwarted in their attempt to rape her. (This is not in the Protestant Bible.)

Bel and the Dragon (or Daniel 14)
Two short tales (not in the Protestant Bible) about the absurdity of idols and the power of the God of Israel.

The Prayer of Azariah and The Song of the Three Young Men (sometimes The Song of the Three Children or The Song of the Three Jews)
Purportedly the songs and prayers uttered by the three young men who were thrown into the burning fiery furnace. (It is not in the Protestant Bible.)

Hosea
Prophecies from the eighth century BC, the century after Elijah and Elisha.

Joel
Penitential poems in a time of natural disaster, but also prophecies of a glorious future when God will 'pour out [his] spirit on all flesh'.

Amos
Prophecies of a contemporary of Hosea, almost entirely doom-laden.

Obadiah
A short prophecy about the punishment of Edom for assisting in the overthrow of Jerusalem in 587 BC.

Jonah
Well-known story about a reluctant prophet swallowed by a fish in punishment for refusing to obey God's command – but set free to go and preach to Nineveh and bring about its repentance.

Micah
Prophecies of a contemporary of Isaiah.

Nahum
Oracles about the divine destruction of Nineveh.

Habakkuk
Prophecies about the coming destruction of Jerusalem, by a contemporary of Jeremiah.

Zephaniah
Condemnations of much in the life of pre-exilic Judah.

Haggai
Words of a prophet who encouraged the community that returned from Exile to rebuild the Temple.

Zechariah
Oracles from a contemporary of Haggai, also concerned with the restoration of the post-exilic community.

Malachi

Attacks on various abuses in the post-exilic community, together with a famous passage predicting the return of Elijah to inaugurate the 'day of the Lord'.

The books from Isaiah to Malachi are usually called the prophetic books.

1 Maccabees

An account of the wars fought by the Jews against the pagan king Antiochus Epiphanes, in the second century BC.

2 Maccabees

A more popular and legendary account of the events recorded in 1 Maccabees, especially the martyrdom of loyal Jews at this time.

THE APOCRYPHA

Some Protestant Bibles include the books that are not regarded as properly a part of the Old Testament in an appendix called 'The Apocrypha'. This involves presenting the additions to Daniel (Susannah, Bel and the Dragon and the Song of the Three Children) as if they were three separate books. The Additions to Esther (see above) are fragmentary, and so make no continuous sense when removed from the book itself, as can be seen by looking at a copy of the Apocrypha. Protestant Apocryphas also contain three works not normally included in Catholic Bibles at all:

1 Esdras A reworked version of parts of Chronicles, Ezra, and Nehemiah.

2 Esdras A partly Christian work from the first century AD.

The Prayer of Manasseh A penitential text.

Greek and other Eastern Orthodox Bibles in some cases have further additions.

THE NEW TESTAMENT

Matthew
The Gospel according to Matthew places emphasis on the teachings of Jesus, and includes (Chapters 5—7) the Sermon on the Mount.

Mark
Mark is the shortest Gospel, and contains very little that is not also in one of the others.

Luke
The longest Gospel, Luke contains many parables and stories peculiar to itself, such as the parables of the prodigal son and the good Samaritan, and the account of the walk to Emmaus.

These three Gospels are sometimes called the Synoptic Gospels – i.e. Gospels sharing a similar perspective.

John
John (or 'the Fourth Gospel') is radically different from the Synoptics. Jesus' teaching centres on his own identity – hence the many 'I am' sayings – and most of the parables are missing.

The Acts of the Apostles
Apparently the second volume of Luke, this consists of an account of the history of the early Church, and especially of the missions conducted by Paul around the Mediterranean.

Romans
Paul's longest letter is to a church he did not found and had never visited. It is concerned predominantly with the relationship of Jews and Gentiles in the Church, and with the question of the basis for salvation – obedience to the Jewish law or faith in Christ?

1 Corinthians
Corinth was a large and sophisticated city, and Paul's first letter to the Christians there is largely concerned with how they should relate to the society around them, and how the church should organise its own affairs. 'The foolishness of God is wiser than human wisdom.'

2 Corinthians
This deals further with relationships within the Corinthian church, and also responds to challenges to Paul's own authority.

Galatians
The only letter not to begin by congratulating the recipients on their faith, Galatians (like Romans) deals with the theme of 'justification by faith', but in an atmosphere of anger and hostility to what Paul sees as the Galatians' errors.

Ephesians
Possibly in origin an encyclical, intended for general circulation (not all manuscripts mention Ephesus), this is a rather systematic treatment of various theological themes. There is some overlap with Colossians.

Philippians
Paul's most gently 'pastoral' letter, evidently written from prison to encourage the Christians in Philippi to loyalty and generosity.

Colossians
One of the most extended statements of Paul's Christology (teaching about the nature of Jesus). The letter also tries to dissuade the Christians at Colossae from subscribing to a system of 'philosophy' which is incompatible with Christian faith, according to the writer.

1 Thessalonians
Probably Paul's earliest letter, this deals especially with themes of eschatology (God's plan for history and the role of Jesus in bringing in the end-time).

2 Thessalonians
Further eschatological themes.

1 Timothy
Pastoral advice to Timothy, who was apparently appointed by Paul as a leader in Ephesus – almost a bishop, in the later sense.

2 Timothy
Further advice on how to live as the pastor of a Christian community.

Titus
Titus seems to have had a similar role to Timothy's, but in Crete, and is similarly advised by Paul to live soberly and discreetly.

The three epistles – 1 and 2 Timothy and Titus – are generally called the Pastoral Epistles. It is widely thought that they are imitations of Paul's genuine letters, and come from a time well after Paul's death.

Philemon
Paul's fourth letter to an individual is the most personal of all, dealing with the problem of a runaway slave, Onesimus.

Hebrews
Some manuscripts attribute this to Paul, but others do not. It seems to be a treatise on the status of Jesus, the Christian life, and the hope of salvation. There is much discussion of various Old Testament texts (not common in Paul's epistles).

James
A collection of ethical teaching.

1 Peter
Themes of baptism and resurrection characterise this work, so much so that some think it was originally an Easter homily.

2 Peter
Almost entirely concerned with eschatological themes, this epistle has much material in common with Jude.

1 John
There are many themes common to 1 John and John's Gospel, including the love which Christians should show to each other as a response to God's love for them, demonstrated in Christ.

2 John
A warning against the dangers of doctrinal error.

3 John
A short pastoral letter dealing with a problem of discipline in the early Church.

Jude
A denunciation of 'error' in the Church, with threats based on eschatological ideas shared with 2 Peter.

Revelation
An apocalyptic work concerned with the end-time and the role of Christ in the new world which will follow the end.

The letters from 1 Peter to Jude are sometimes called the general or catholic epistles, because they were felt to be addressed to all Christians, as opposed to Paul's, which are to specific communities.

CHAPTER TWO

Writing the Books

WRITING IN THE BIBLICAL WORLD

Writing was practised in the Middle East long before the time when Israel came into existence as a nation. Literacy was not widespread in most ancient cultures, but in all the states from Mesopotamia to Egypt there were professional scribes or writers, as well as literate people following other occupations, from at least the middle of the third millennium BC (2500 or so). Even if the beginnings of Hebrew culture are set as early as 1700 BC (a traditional date for the birth of Abraham, though almost certainly too early by some centuries), the world of the Bible was a world of writing from start to finish.

From at least the time of King Solomon (perhaps *c.* 970 – *c.* 930 BC), the people of Israel lived a settled existence, in cities, towns, and villages. In this context there were places to store books, and opportunities for preparing the writing-materials (usually papyrus) out of which books were made. The picture-book idea of the Israelites as bedouin living a nomadic life in tents, unable to record anything in writing, is quite untrue to the historical reality, even for this early period.

Hebrew culture had one particularly valuable aid to reading and writing: the alphabet. Mesopotamian culture down into the first millennium BC used cuneiform writing, in which signs representing syllables were incised into clay tablets with a wedge-shaped stylus. The Phoenicians first developed, in place of this syllabic writing, an alphabetic system – the ancestor of the Hebrew alphabet and ultimately of our own – in which each symbol stands for a single consonant. The result is a much simpler system, in which the several hundred characters of cuneiform are replaced with just 22 letters of the alphabet, making reading and writing much easier, accessible even to non-professionals. All the books of the Old Testament are written in this alphabetic script, which changed in its detailed style over the years but never deviated from the basic 22 letters. In all probability some parts of the Old Testament are as old as the tenth or eleventh century BC – the poem in Judges 5 is usually acclaimed as the oldest text in the Bible – while the latest, Daniel, comes from the middle of the second century (160 BC or so).

The New Testament is even more clearly the product of a literate culture. The Mediterranean world by the time of Jesus had libraries, book shops, and many professional writers and translators. The Greek in which the New Testament is written is mostly the everyday Greek used by educated people of the time – a type of Greek which had become the common language of the whole Mediterranean area, including much of Italy, where it was used alongside Latin. Writers often employed professional scribes to take down their words, often in shorthand, and St Paul's letter to the Romans includes a greeting from Paul's amanuensis or secretary, Gaius (Rom. 16:22). On a number of occasions Paul adds a greeting in his own hand to authenticate the letter (like a modern signature at the end of a typed letter) – implying that the rest of the letter was written down for him (see 1 Cor. 16:21, Gal. 6:11, Col. 4:18, 2 Thess. 3:17).

Thus the world of the Bible was a world of writing and of books to a far greater extent than people today generally realise. To understand the Bible it is necessary to see it as the product of skilful writers who can be compared with other writers of the ancient and modern worlds.

WHO WROTE THE SCRIPTURES?

But who were these writers? To a great extent, biblical books are anonymous. The main exceptions are St Paul's epistles, which begin (as letters did at that time) with his name, and then go on to identify the addressees: 'Paul, called by the will of God to be an apostle of Christ Jesus, and our brother Sosthenes, to the church of God which is at Corinth . . . grace to you and peace' (1 Cor. 1.1–3). The other New Testament epistles also begin with the name of a sender, as does the book of Revelation, which is formally also a set of letters, at least in its opening chapters. But the attribution of the Gospels to Matthew, Mark, Luke, and John, appears only in the headings (in the Greek simply, 'According to Mark', etc., without the word 'Gospel').

In the Old Testament even the names that do appear in the present titles of the books are seldom a claim about authorship. The book of Job, for example, is a book *about* Job, not a book *by* Job; the same is probably true of 'the First and Second Books of Samuel' (though people in antiquity sometimes thought they were by Samuel, despite containing the news of his death). We often call the first five books of the Old Testament (the Pentateuch) 'the books of Moses', but they are not said to be by Moses anywhere within the text itself – the most that can be said is that Moses is supposed to have written some parts, such as the laws in Exodus 34.11–26: see Exodus 34.27–8, 'And the LORD said to Moses, "Write these words" . . . and he wrote upon the tables the words of the covenant.' The 'Psalms of David' and the 'Proverbs of Solomon' may not mean 'the Psalms/Proverbs which David/Solomon *wrote*', so much as 'the Psalms/Proverbs *belonging to* David/ Solomon'. And no one has ever taken the title 'The First and Second Books of the Kings' to be anything other than a statement of subject-matter.

But there is a more far-reaching reason why it is hard to say who wrote the biblical books. This is that very few of them are simple texts composed by just one person at one time. For example, we tend to think of Genesis as the first book of the Bible, and so in an obvious sense it is. But if we ask whether it was also the first book to be written, we face a complex problem.

It seems obvious, with any writer's works, to ask in what order they were written – and there is usually at least a plausible answer. Even if there is not enough evidence to be sure, at least the question is a sensible and coherent one. But Genesis, and many other biblical books, contain sections that come from many different periods. They are like scrapbooks or anthologies. This can be seen from some inconsistencies within the story being told. For instance, in Genesis 4:26 we learn that 'men began to call on the name of the LORD' – that is, to worship God by his special Hebrew name YHWH* – in the days of Enosh, Adam's grandson. But in the account of Moses' life in Exodus 6:2–3, it appears that this name was still unknown until the time of Moses, who was commissioned to disclose it to his fellow Israelites. Similarly, Genesis

---

* The Hebrew alphabet originally indicated only consonants – rather like some forms of shorthand. We think that the name of God was probably pronounced 'Yahweh' in ancient times. By the New Testament period, however, people had stopped pronouncing it altogether, for reasons of reverence, and when reading Scripture aloud substituted 'Adonai', which means 'my Lord'. When indications of the vowels of Hebrew were eventually devised, the consonants YHWH were written with the vowels of Adonai. The result is actually an impossible Hebrew word – which helps to signal that the vowels are just a reminder to say 'Adonai'. In Christianity, however, the impossible name came to be read as written, yielding (roughly) Yahowah – the 'Jehovah' of English Bibles, a name by which God was never called in Judaism. The normal convention now is to substitute 'the Lord' wherever the name YHWH occurs, but to print it in capitals and small capitals: 'The LORD'.

1:24–7 asserts that the animals were created before human beings, whereas Genesis 2:18–19 sees man as having been created first, then the animals to be companions for him. There are so many cases like these that scholars have generally concluded that Genesis, Exodus, and most other books in the Old Testament, are 'composite', formed from materials coming from many different periods and settings. But if this is so, then there was no 'author' of Genesis at all in our sense of the term – at best, there was a compiler who combined the material at his disposal. If this is true of all or most of the books in the Bible, then dating the books and arranging them in chronological order becomes not just a difficult task, but a task that is impossible in principle, even a meaningless task.

Compiling a book from pre-existing materials seems strange to most modern people, but it does still happen. A good example is the diary of Anne Frank, the Jewish girl who lived in hiding with her family in Amsterdam for two years, until she was discovered by the German authorities in 1944 and sent to her death at Bergen-Belsen. This is how the translator of the 1997 edition of the diary describes the stages through which *The Diary of a Young Girl* passed:

> Anne Frank decided that when the war was over she would publish a book based on her diary. She began rewriting and editing her diary, improving on the text, omitting passages she didn't think were interesting enough and adding others from memory. At the same time, she kept up her original diary. In the scholarly work *The Diary of Anne Frank: The Critical Edition* (1989), Anne's first, unedited diary is referred to as version *a*, to distinguish it from her second, edited diary, which is known as version *b* . . .

After long deliberation, Otto Frank decided to fulfil his daughter's wish and publish her diary. He selected material from versions *a* and *b*, editing them into a shorter version later referred to as version *c*. Readers all over the world know this as *The Diary of a Young Girl*.

The Anne Frank-Fonds (Anne Frank Foundation) in Basle (Switzerland), which as Otto Frank's sole heir had also inherited his daughter's copyrights, then decided to have a new, expanded edition of the diary published for general readers . . . Otto Frank's original selection has now been supplemented with passages from Anne's *a* and *b* versions.*

If this degree of complexity can be found in preparing for publication what is basically a single document with one author, then it is not surprising that the creation of some of the biblical books is of a different order of magnitude. This can be seen by examining the Gospels.

THE GOSPELS

In an obvious sense all four Gospels tell the same story. They present an account of how Jesus of Nazareth gathered disciples, taught and healed, and then fell foul of the authorities and was tried, crucified, and buried, but subsequently rose from the dead. However, as soon as we try to flesh out the details, we find that the Gospels often contradict each other. Did the 'cleansing of the Temple' occur at the beginning of Jesus' public activity (John 2:13–22), or towards its end (Matt. 12:12–13, and similarly in Mark and Luke)? When Jesus was asked, 'Good

---

* Anne Frank, *The Diary of a Young Girl*, (new translation, ed. Otto H. Frank and Mirjam Pressler), London, Viking, 1997.

Teacher, what must I do to inherit eternal life?', did he reply, 'Why do you call me good?' (Mark 10:18) or 'Why do you ask me about what is good?' (Matt. 19:17)? More crucially, perhaps, did Jesus teach mainly about how people ought to live, as in Matthew, Mark, and Luke, or mainly about his own status and place in God's plan for the world, as in John?

The attempt to untangle some of these problems has led to a consensus that John stands somewhat apart from the other, 'Synoptic' Gospels. Among the Synoptics, there is much shared material and yet many differences, and the best hypothesis seems to be that there is some degree of interdependence, combined with a shared use of documents or collections of Jesus' sayings which are now lost. Most, though not all, New Testament scholars believe that Mark was the first Gospel to be compiled – but out of diverse materials already collected by others! – and that Matthew and Luke used both Mark (in some form or other), along with a collection of the sayings of Jesus conventionally known as Q. This implies a task of collection, selection, and compilation which would mean that none of the Gospels was complete until some 30 or 40 years at least after Jesus' death – though much of the material in them would, of course, be a great deal earlier, and much might go back to Jesus' first disciples.

Studying the Synoptic Gospels leads to a further insight, which makes it even harder to attempt to establish the date of biblical books. As we have just seen, the date of a Gospel is not necessarily the same as the date of the material it contains, since even in a Gospel written in, say, AD 70, 40 years on from the life of Jesus himself, there may be sayings of Jesus, or anecdotes about him, which are factually true, that is, which really are what he said or did. They may have been faithfully preserved in documents, now lost, much older than our present Gospels.

According to one school of thought, Jesus' disciples actually wrote down his sayings themselves, so that the evangelists or Gospel-writers were drawing on material as authentic as anything could be. On the other hand, there could in principle be material in the Gospels which the evangelists themselves made up from scratch. Some critics think that the Nativity stories in Luke 1—2 are an example of this – legends composed by analogy with Old Testament stories about great heroes, which never had any basis in fact at all. Thus the date and truth of the Gospels' content is a very involved question.

There is a complicating factor here. It is possible that the material used by the evangelists had been handed down, not in writing, but by word of mouth. Perhaps Gospel-writers were not drawing on written materials, but on oral memory. Large claims are sometimes made for the ability of people in traditional cultures to learn material by heart, remember it and hand it down by word of mouth – and some scholars think that the Gospels rest substantially on that kind of activity. The problem is that oral material is much harder to check than written documents, and it is hard to see how it could avoid being changed, undetectably, in the transmission.

A whole school of New Testament scholarship – form criticism – takes it for granted that the Gospel sayings and stories were handed on orally. The main occasion for this would have been the Church's worship. Each week, perhaps, a story about Jesus was recounted to Christians who assembled for worship, first by those who had known him and then by those who had known them. The intention would have been to pass on truly what the Lord had said. But little by little stories would have taken on the flavour of the Christian community in which they were told, and would have been accommodated to its needs and problems. For example, stories of Jesus' conflicts with opponents within Judaism gradually acquired a sharper edge as the Church found itself increasingly in dispute with other Jews, and eventually excluded from the Jewish fold altogether. The presentation of 'scribes' and 'Pharisees' in the Synoptic Gospels, and of 'the Jews' in general in John, would then reflect this later conflict rather than the much less stark opposition to the Jewish authorities by Jesus himself. To some extent, however, we may be able to reconstruct the process of this development, and so get back to a more authentic presentation of Jesus and his teaching than any of the Gospels now contains.

On the other hand, if the materials in the Gospels had already changed and developed before the evangelists came by them, we ought to allow for the possibility that they themselves made deliberate changes – that they were more than mere compilers. The usual term in biblical studies for a compiler who makes creative changes to the material he has inherited is 'redactor', and the study of what redactors do is known as 'redaction criticism'. Redaction critics, though entirely aware that the Gospel-writers were not composing freely but had sources (either written or oral), maintain that they also contributed much themselves. Perhaps there is not all that much difference between calling Matthew, Mark, Luke and John redactors and calling them authors, since each writer adapted the material he had received in such a way as to impose his own characteristic stamp on it. The Lucan Jesus is in important ways different from the Matthaean one. For example, in Luke, Jesus sits loosely to the law of Moses, but is deeply concerned with the poor and other disadvantaged groups in society; whereas in Matthew, he intensifies the stringency of the law, and is interested much more in problems inside the Church. The best way to explain this might be to think of the two evangelists in question as having a different agenda in their own church setting, different problems to confront and different dangers against which to warn their readers.

Thus the issue of when and how the Gospels were written turns out to be very intricate. To simplify, though, we might say that there definitely was an end-point to the process – a point after which the Gospel was not edited any further; and this end-point can be specified very roughly for each Gospel. Mark was the first to be completed, possibly before the fall of Jerusalem to the Romans in AD 70, but probably not long after. Matthew and Luke come from a decade or more later, and John comes from the very end of the first century – so at least the general consensus of New Testament scholars holds. But if by the date of writing we mean the date by which the material was first written down at all, then for some parts of it there are much earlier possibilities, conceivably going back to the time of Jesus himself. And if some was transmitted orally, then any date is more or less arbitrary, since the material was slowly and gradually moulded and changed over time, and we could say with equal validity that it comes from the 40s, 50s, 60s, or 70s AD, none of these dates representing a definitive point.

THE LETTERS

The epistles or letters in the New Testament present a very different problem. Writing a letter is a different process from compiling a historical narrative. It is a matter of conveying a message as clearly as possible, not of weaving together all sorts of fragmentary information and shaping it to form an ordered whole. The question of how, and when, Paul's epistles came to be written is not in principle difficult (though in fact we sometimes lack the necessary historical information to make us certain). We know from Acts, and indeed from Paul's letters themselves, that he went on several long journeys around the Mediterranean, either creating churches in places where the gospel had not yet been preached or building up churches which he had founded on a previous journey. Piecing together the historical indications in both Acts and the epistles, it is possible to establish a probable chronological order for the letters: 1 and 2 Thessalonians, 1 and 2 Corinthians, Galatians, Romans, Philippians, Colossians, Philemon, Ephesians, 1 and 2 Timothy, Titus.

It is with the epistles, however, that we meet the problem of *pseudonymity*. Most of the time, as we have seen, biblical books do not tell us who wrote them; but on the rather rare occasions when they do, they are sometimes not telling the truth! Most critics agree that the Pastoral Epistles – 1 and 2 Timothy and Titus – invoke Paul's name and authority, but are really by a second-generation leader in one of the churches founded by Paul. Ephesians is widely thought to be a kind of encyclical letter, and to belong to the stage when Paul's letters were being collected to form a set (see Chapter 3 below). Some scholars also doubt the authenticity of Colossians, which is closely related to Ephesians in theme. Pseudonymity is hard to understand in a culture such as ours, which sets great store on authenticating documents, because it appears simply deceitful, and seems to detract from the religious integrity of the works in question. In the ancient world, the use of other people's names was a more subtle matter: there were legitimate as well as illicit cases. We shall return to this in the next chapter. If the genuine Pauline letters come from the period up to about AD 60, then the 'deutero-Paulines' are presumably substantially later, from the second half of the first century or even into the second. In them Paul has become not just the founder of churches but the person who gave them their shape and order, and from whom the leaders ('bishops') derive their authority. And there is something that can be called 'the faith', a body of tradition which Paul had handed over to the leaders and which they must defend – an idea typical of writers in the second century but not clearly of Paul himself.

The remaining epistles in the New Testament are for the most part likewise pseudonymous, except for one that is anonymous: Hebrews. As we shall see, many people in the early Church assumed that Hebrews was by Paul, and it still appears as 'the Epistle of Paul the Apostle to the Hebrews' in the Authorised Version. But it does not begin with any author's name, and Origen, a theologian of the early third century (*c*. 185–*c*. 254), already saw that its style was so different from that of Paul that it could not be by him. In fact even the designation 'epistle' seems foreign to its character. It is more like a short treatise than a letter, though towards the end (see 13:22) the author does adopt some of the conventions of a letter. There is an old speculation that the author was the evangelist Luke; in recent times another suggested author has been Paul's friend and colleague Apollos. It too – along with the epistles of John, Peter and James – is a second-generation document, by comparison with the works of Paul. While 2 and 3 John seem to be genuinely epistles, addressed to a concrete situation (a breakdown in church order), the others seem to adopt the letter-form artificially, perhaps because of the prestige Paul had conferred on it.

DATING THE OLD TESTAMENT

From a modern perspective, 2,000 years on from the beginnings of Christianity, it may seem almost nit-picking to debate whether a particular New Testament document comes from AD 50, 70, or 90. We may feel that, whatever the exact truth, all these works are close enough to Jesus to have a strong claim on the attention of a Christian. But of course a great deal can change in the space of 40 or 50 years, and a comparison between the earliest New Testament writing (1 Thessalonians) and later material (such as Titus or 2 Peter) shows a substantial shift in the understanding of the essence of Christian faith and allegiance. Nevertheless, the time-span involved is certainly short. If we now return to the Old Testament, we find that much greater periods of time are involved, as well as a far greater variety of literary types.

The prophets

A good place to start is the books of the prophets. The prophets may have been literate – several of them (e.g. Isaiah, Jeremiah, Ezekiel) came from educated circles, the latter two being priests. But they probably did not write down their speeches and sayings, but delivered them orally. When Jeremiah is told by God to get his secretary, Baruch, to write down his oracles (Jer. 36), it sounds as though this is something unusual. So how do we come to have prophetic books at all? The usual answer is that the prophets' disciples learned many of their sayings by heart, and then transmitted them, either orally or in writing, to *their* disciples, until eventually a book of the sayings of this or that prophet took shape.

But in the process of transmission a good deal may have been changed or lost. There are various passages in the prophetic books which seem unlikely to go back to the prophets themselves. For example, there are anachronistic references. The book of Amos ends (9:11–15) with a prediction of the glorious restoration of the fallen house of David – in other words, of the dynasty in the southern Hebrew kingdom, Judah. This is the only oracle in Amos promising blessings – the book is otherwise extremely gloomy – but, more important, it presupposes that the house of David has fallen. This was not so in Amos's day, when Judah was a prosperous nation ruled by Uzziah, a descendant of David. It seems to most commentators likely that a later disciple of the prophet (or editor of the book – it is hard to tell which) added the oracle as a 'happy ending'.

The most extreme case of editorial activity on the words of the prophets is the book of Isaiah. The prophet Isaiah lived and worked in the eighth century BC, not long after Amos. Yet the book that carries his name has extensive sections which seem to presuppose the sixth century, the time when some Jews were exiled to Babylon by Nebuchadnezzar and then, 60 or 70 years later (in the 530s) allowed to return and rebuild the ruined Temple in Jerusalem. Since the late nineteenth century it has been usual to call Isaiah 40—55, which deals with the plight of the exiles, 'Deutero-Isaiah', that is, the Second Isaiah, and 56—66 'Trito-Isaiah', Third Isaiah, since it is a third section added after the return and rebuilding. Furthermore, even in the book which remains (Isaiah 1—39), many passages imply a time much later than that of Isaiah: much of 24—27, for example, may be later even than Deutero-Isaiah and Trito-Isaiah. The upshot of all this is that the book of Isaiah emerges as a complicated anthology of prophecies, some authentically by Isaiah, but others written in later generations. Was there a 'school' of Isaiah which preserved and added to Isaiah's own compositions? Some scholars think so. Others believe that the book as it stands is the work of editors who had no special connection with Isaiah, but who also worked on other prophetic books – Jeremiah, say, or Ezekiel – for both of those books also have lengthy sections unlikely to go back as far as the time of the prophets themselves.

Dividing the prophetic books into 'authentic' and 'inauthentic' sections is one of the most difficult tasks in Old Testament scholarship, and there is always a slight doubt as to whether it is worth doing. From a religious point of view, it can be said that passages not genuinely by this or that prophet himself are still part of Scripture. And from a more literary perspective, it may be felt that there is more profit in studying the book of Isaiah, as it is, than the dubious fragments which remain after critics have been at work. But if we want to know about Isaiah – the real man of that name – then there is no alternative to this kind of analysis. Furthermore, there are great successes to report – and one being the discovery of Second Isaiah, whose theology (once we consider it on its own, and not as an aspect of Isaiah's) is among the most important contributions to what the Old Testament has to say on the subjects of creation, monotheism and suffering.

Here we can see something which has been implicit in much that has been said so far. We draw a distinction between *writing* books and *collecting* them: in our context, it is obvious that writing a book and creating a library are two quite different tasks. Where ancient Israelite literature is concerned – and even in some measure with the Gospels – the dividing-line between the two activities is much more fluid. Isaiah probably 'wrote' nothing, if we take the word literally: we owe our knowledge of what he said to his disciples. But we cannot say that the book is simply the work of those disciples, since it has been added to over a space of many years, perhaps of several centuries. Deutero-Isaiah and Trito-Isaiah may have been authors in a more literal sense than Isaiah himself – though with them too it may be that we have their words through the work of disciples. But compiling the finished 'Book of Isaiah' was more a work of editorship than of authorship. Yet the editors may have contributed their own distinctive ideas by the way they arranged the material, or by inserting comments of their own, so that the work is not a *mere* anthology. It is important to hold on to this point, which will become critical when we turn, in the next chapter, to the way in which biblical books have been collected into groups. The activities of compiling and collecting books are less sharply divided from the activity of writing books than they would be in the modern world.

Scribes and 'wisdom literature'

We do not know who the writers of the prophetic books actually were. Disciples have been suggested, as we have seen: obviously, literate disciples. But those responsible may instead have been scribes – learned people who wrote for a living, whether as freelancers or as employees of the state or the religious establishment. Other cultures of the time did have such professionals, from whose number the civil service (well-developed both in Egypt and in Mesopotamian states by the second millennium) was largely staffed. It is important to realise how speculative such questions are where the Old Testament is concerned. We know it got written, but we hardly ever know who wrote it.

Perhaps the major candidate for composition by professional scribes is the book of Proverbs. Some think that a collection of the 'Proverbs of Solomon' really could go back to Solomon's own day, that the wisdom tradition embodied in that book began at his court and was fostered by his scribes. Certainly books like Proverbs existed in Egypt and in Mesopotamia, and in some cases at least seem to have been the literature of such learned scribes. Some of the biblical proverbs do seem to belong at court:

When you sit down to eat with a ruler,
>   observe carefully what is before you;
> and put a knife to your throat
>   if you are a man given to appetite.
> Do not desire his delicacies,
>   for they are deceptive food.

(Prov. 23:1–3)

But others represent the wisdom of the village:

> A righteous man has regard for the life of his beast,
>   but the mercy of the wicked is cruel.
> He who tills his land will have plenty of bread,
>   but he who follows worthless pursuits has no
>   sense.

(Prov. 12:10–11)

Proverbs such as these have no authors in the ordinary sense. But they may well have been *collected* by professional scribes. It must be said that the date of Proverbs as a collection is essentially unknown, since its contents relate observations on life of such a general kind that almost any period in which the classical Hebrew language was in use – say, 1100 BC to 300 BC – could be a candidate. And, as usual, there is every reason to think that the book has passed through several editions, much as the prophetic books have done.

Narrative

Half of the Old Testament is made up of narrative or (in a loose sense) histories. The Pentateuch was discussed briefly above. Not everyone agrees with the hypothesis that it was composed by weaving sources together, though this is still the classic theory from which most biblical studies begin. But almost everyone thinks that it is com-

posite – not composed straight through in one piece – and
that it, too, has gone through several editorial stages. In a
passage such as the following, it is hard to think that we
have the coherent work of only one writer:

> Then Moses and Aaron, Nadab, and Abihu, and
> seventy of the elders of Israel went up, and they saw
> the God of Israel; and there was under his feet as it
> were a pavement of sapphire stone, like the very
> heaven for clearness. And he did not lay his hand on
> the chief men of the people of Israel; they beheld God,
> and ate and drank.
>
> The LORD said to Moses, 'Come up to me on the
> mountain, and wait there; and I will give you the
> tables of stone, with the law and the commandment,
> which I have written for their instruction.' So Moses
> rose with his servant Joshua, and Moses went up into
> the mountain of God. And he said to the elders, 'Tarry
> here for us, until we come to you again; and behold,
> Aaron and Hur are with you; whoever has a cause, let
> him go to them.'
>
> Then Moses went up on the mountain, and the cloud
> covered the mountain. The glory of the LORD settled on
> Mount Sinai, and the cloud covered it six days; and
> on the seventh day he called to Moses out of the midst
> of the cloud. Now the appearance of the glory of the
> LORD was like a devouring fire on the top of the moun-
> tain in the sight of the people of Israel. And Moses
> entered the cloud, and went up on the mountain.
>
> (Exod. 24:9–18)

Provided we look at the scene here through a very soft
focus, we get a general impression of Moses' encounter
with God. But if we try to work out in detail what is
happening, as we would need to do if, for example, we
were trying to film it, we start to see that it is fairly

incoherent. How many times does Moses go up the mountain? Did he come down again in between? Who was actually with him, and where were 'the people of Israel'? People who have studied this text, and similar ones, in detail have usually come to the conclusion that they are the work of more than one 'author' – perhaps different versions of the same story, which a later editor has welded together. But the identity of any of the writers remains a mystery.

A lot of work has been done in studying the historical books from Joshua to 2 Kings, and also the books of Chronicles, Ezra and Nehemiah. It is fairly well established that the books from Joshua to 2 Kings were written/compiled during the Exile of the sixth century BC, and are meant to explain and describe Israel's decline from its successful settlement of the land of Canaan, through the empire of David and Solomon, to the disaster of the Exile. To do this the writers/compilers have drawn on a vast range of already existing material – from official royal annals (such as the 'book of the chronicles of the kings of Judah', 2 Kings 21:25, or the 'book of the acts of Solomon', 1 Kings 11:41) all the way to popular legends – subordinating it to a consistent dating-scheme and shaping it to make various theological points about Israel's destiny. 1 and 2 Chronicles retell much of this story from a post-exilic perspective (some time in the fifth century BC), while Ezra and Nehemiah preserve rather fragmentary accounts of the post-exilic reconstruction and so must be no earlier than the late fifth or fourth century BC.

In the case of Joshua — 2 Kings there may be a clue as to the identity of the writers. Many of the work's theological themes are close to ideas in the book of Deuteronomy, a collection of laws generally thought to have been put in their final form during the seventh century BC — less than a century before the historians produced their account. For this reason the history-work Joshua — 2 Kings is widely referred to in academic biblical studies as the Deuteronomistic History. This justifies the hypothesis that the authors/compilers may have been close to the compilers of Deuteronomy itself – in other words, some group of people concerned with the administration or teaching of the law: prophets, priests and professional scribes have all been proposed at one time or another.

Works with authors

Finally, there are a few books in the Old Testament which can be said to have an author in the same sense as Paul's epistles – they are the work of one writer composing freely and with a point to make. The books of Ruth and Jonah, short stories about imaginary characters, have few signs of being compilations. They seem to be conscious works of fiction, and probably date from well after the Exile. Ecclesiastes is presented as, and probably really is, the work of 'Qoheleth' ('the Preacher' in the Authorised Version), though it sometimes seems to quote earlier proverbs. Job as a whole is composite, if the usual view is right which sees the prose Prologue and Epilogue (1—2 and 42:7–17) as coming from a different hand from the verse dialogue in 3:1—42:6. But that dialogue itself has all the signs of stemming from a creative writer who was composing, not assembling older fragments; it too comes from no earlier than the fifth century BC.

CONCLUSION: A TANGLED TALE

This has not been a comprehensive guide to the books of the Bible: some books have not been mentioned, and many theories about them have been glossed over. The purpose of the survey has been twofold:

1. I have tried to show the complexity of the process by which all these books came to be fixed in writing. Some were unified written texts from the beginning, written or at least dictated by one person. The obvious cases of this are the epistles of Paul, but a few Old Testament books come into the same category – Ruth and Ecclesiastes have just been mentioned. At the other extreme, some books seem to have been put together like a mosaic from scattered fragments. The Pentateuch is seen in this way by some, but Proverbs might be a better example. In between are the great majority of books, where an editor or series of editors have taken material that already existed (either orally or in writing) and have used it to create a relatively coherent work, where some undarned ends can still be seen, but in which a consistent pattern emerges none the less. The Deuteronomistic History is a classic case of this; so are the Gospels. Because the final redactor has moulded the material he received in a consistent way, each of the Gospels has its own distinctive character, despite the fact that they all share a certain amount of source-material. If we have studied the Gospels in detail, we know at once, if we are presented with an unidentified passage, which Gospel it is likely to be from. This means that the Gospel-writers, even if not 'authors' in our sense, are much more than copy-typists simply transcribing what they have found in earlier sources.

2. As already hinted, I want to stress the lack of clear distinction between writing and collecting in the cultures which produced the Bible. Older doctrines of biblical inspiration that talk of God inspiring 'the bib-

lical authors' are difficult to apply to the historical situation as we have described it. It is not simply that there are only a few real authors and the rest are compilers: it is that authorship seems often to be *conceived* as a kind of compilation – or, if you prefer, that compilation was the only kind of authorship some people knew. The 'author' of Proverbs was simply a compiler, though he may have compiled creatively, placing the material he had inherited in the right order to get across whatever points he wanted to make. The compiler of the Pentateuch was a creative author, welding heterogeneous material into a finished whole.

The biblical world was not familiar with many of our distinctions. The Hebrew word *sopher*, 'scribe' or 'writer', covered a much wider range than our words 'writer' or 'author' – in fact, 'secretary' might be a better translation of it. In the English civil service, Secretaries of State have Private Secretaries (civil servants who act as their personal helpers), but both the Secretaries of State and the Private Secretaries have secretaries – that is, people to handle their papers and do their typing. In Hebrew, *sopher* has roughly the same range of meanings – from someone who carries out the chore of copying neatly what others have composed, to someone who has secretaries to whom he can dictate and who therefore probably 'writes' rather little, in the literal sense of the term. Furthermore, there is no way of distinguishing between a writer in the modern sense of an 'author', and a writer in the sense of someone skilled in mixing ink and smoothing out papyrus. The Graeco-Roman world did draw this distinction, but even there it is less sharp than we make it.

When in the next chapter we move on, from gathering

material to make books, to gathering books to make larger collections, we need to have these fuzzy thoughts rather firmly in mind.

CHAPTER THREE

Collecting the Books

For there to be a Bible, it is not enough that a lot of books should have existed, in ancient Israel or in the early Church. They need to have been collected, to form a 'corpus'. In the Bible as we know it, the collection is bound together in the most literal way: all the biblical books form a single volume, much as do the different chapters in a novel. We have to remind ourselves of the different technology for book-production in the ancient world. In Israel, as in classical Greece and Rome, a book was written on one side of a very long strip of papyrus or, sometimes, leather, which was then rolled up to form a scroll. It had a rigid wooden bar, or 'roller', at each end, so that it could be rolled easily from one end to the other, with one roller held in each hand: the writing was then arranged in quite narrow columns parallel to the rollers. A single scroll could hold only about as much writing as there is in the book of Isaiah.

A collection of books, in this context, would have to mean precisely that: a collection, not a single volume of collected works. 'The Bible' would have been, as it were, not the name of a book but the name of a small library. (Indeed, the word 'bible' derives from the Greek *biblia*, which is a plural, meaning 'books'.) This ancient pattern persists to this day in the synagogue, where the five books of Moses (Genesis to Deuteronomy) are still written on five scrolls, kept in a cupboard called the 'ark', and brought out each sabbath for ceremonial reading. But for all other purposes Jews, like Christians, use a single volume or codex for the Bible.

In the ancient world the codex – what we call simply a book, a volume bound flat with two covers and a spine – came into being in around the first century AD; and it has a close, but as yet unexplained, connection with Christianity. Though there were scrolls of the Gospels and epistles, from very early on Christians adopted the codex for their own books, and soon began to write the Old Testament in codices, too. One possible motive may have been the desire to be different from the Jews. Another may have been that they regarded the Gospels as notes from which a preacher could retell the stories of Jesus, rather than as polished literary 'works', and so adopted the codex which was, in that culture, the equivalent of a notebook – rather as if we were to keep the Gospels scribbled out by hand in a reporter's spiral-bound notebook instead of a leather-bound Bible printed on India paper. But, whatever the cause, this meant that Christians were soon in a position to collect their holy books, not just by storing them in a single room in some kind of order, but by writing them consecutively in a single codex, or a few codices. (A question about the *order* of books in the Bible is thus more easily answered in the case of Christians than of Jews.)

Bearing this difference in mind, we can now ask about the collections which were made of the biblical books in Christianity and in Judaism.

'MOSES'

At around the time of the Exile to Babylonia, one or two editions were produced of what we called above the Deuteronomistic History – the historical books of Joshua, Judges, Samuel and Kings. But there are rival theories about how this historical work is related to the Pentateuch, which also, after all, narrates the history of Israel, down to the place where the Deuteronomistic work picks up the story. The older view, from the late nineteenth to mid twentieth century, was that the Pentateuchal history was really in origin a Hexateuch – a collection of six books (the Greek *hex* means 'six'). The book of Joshua, according to this theory, was originally the sequel to Deuteronomy, recording how the promises made to the Hebrew patriarchs in Genesis were fulfilled when the Promised Land was finally settled under the leadership of Joshua. This Hexateuch would have been an optimistic, up-beat work, ending with the Israelites triumphantly in possession of Palestine.

More recently, scholars have tended instead to see Joshua as an integral part of the Deuteronomistic work, but also to regard the book of Deuteronomy itself as belonging to this work, functioning as its prelude. Deuteronomy sets the scene for the History by making clear what are God's laws and requirements if the people are to enjoy his blessing, and what will be their fate if they disregard them. From the Historian's perspective, in the Exile, this dire prediction had now come true, and so he tried to present the history of the nation as a working out of Deuteronomy's warnings. Probably the core of Deuteronomy had existed before the Exile, but the Historian added much to it, especially the blessings and curses of the later chapters (Deut. 28—30), and the historical prologue in chapters 1—3, which is to be seen as introducing the whole subsequent history-work, not just the book of Deuteronomy. On this second view, then, there was originally a Tetrateuch (a collection of four books, from the Greek *tettara*, meaning 'four') consisting of Genesis, Exodus, Leviticus and Numbers, which ended with the death of Moses.

The curious thing is that neither of these arrangements corresponds to what came to be normative in Judaism.

From at least the fourth century BC Jews regarded the historical content of the Hebrew Bible as divided into the five books of Moses – Genesis, Exodus, Leviticus, Numbers and Deuteronomy – and four books rather confusingly called 'prophets' (on this see below) – Joshua, Judges, Samuel and Kings (Samuel and Kings were not originally divided into two books each). Two motives seem to underlie this. One is a desire to have a set of books which represent the teaching, life and work of Moses. By *this* time, all law-giving was seen as concentrated in the hand of Moses, much as psalm-writing was ascribed to David and wise proverbs to Solomon. The Pentateuch is sometimes referred to in the New Testament as, simply, 'Moses' (e.g. Luke 16:29–31, 24:27; Acts 15:21), and ending the collection with Moses' death must have seemed a natural thing.

Another motive may have been connected with the experience of the Exile. For a people no longer in possession of their own land – even if some of them had been allowed to resettle in it – the optimistic note of Joshua may have rung hollow. By ending the great foundation document of the Jewish religion with the death of Moses, not yet in the Promised Land, they may have been signalling their own experience as exiles and sojourners in lands belonging to others.

For these or whatever other reasons, Judaism saw the books of Moses not as simply the beginning of a story that would continue through Joshua, Judges, and so on, but as a closed, self-contained work in which all the essentials of Jewish faith and life were to be found. From about the time of Ezra, in the fifth century BC, the Pentateuch or 'Torah' (Hebrew for law, instruction, guidance – all these are elements in Torah) was the centrepiece of Jewish identity. No other books equalled it in prestige and holiness. We shall go on (in the next chapter) to discuss the status of the Torah in more depth, but for now note simply that it clearly formed a collection: five scrolls which belonged together and were always kept together.

The first Christians were of course Jews, and presumably saw the Torah as central in the same way as other Jews did – but very soon a different attitude emerged. By the second century AD Christians seem no longer to have made any great distinction between the Pentateuch and other Scriptures, and consequently saw no break between Deuteronomy and Joshua. Some Christian writers began to use words like Enneateuch (from the Greek *ennea*, meaning 'nine') for the nine books of Genesis, Exodus, Leviticus, Numbers, Deuteronomy, Joshua, Judges, Samuel and Kings. Because Christians no longer saw their religion as centred on law but more on Christ, it no longer seemed important to give the books of Moses a specially prominent position. They also, incidentally, tended to ascribe more importance to the book of Joshua, for the simple reason that Joshua in Greek is *Iesous*, 'Jesus' – and a book named after Jesus, even if coincidentally, could hardly be relegated to the second division. Paul still regularly speaks of 'Moses and the prophets', 'the law and the prophets', and many sayings attributed to Jesus in the Gospels also do so. But by the second century this was becoming less common. It occurs as a convention, not because it expresses a distinction that mattered to people.

One factor here is the change from a predominantly Jewish Church to one consisting principally of Gentiles, whose language was Greek, not Hebrew. Indeed, by New Testament times many Jews outside Palestine, and some within it, spoke Greek as their first language. Because of this the Jewish Scriptures existed in a Greek translation. According to legend, it was one of the rulers of Egypt, Ptolemy Philadelphus (285–246 BC), who first commanded that the Torah should be translated into Greek so that he could form his own opinion of the laws of his Jewish subjects and place a copy in the famous library at Alexandria. Seventy (or 72) translators set to work, and soon produced a Greek version: hence it is called the Septuagint (Latin *septuaginta*, meaning 'seventy') or LXX. The reality is that Greek-speaking Jews, especially in Egypt, needed a Greek version of the Scriptures themselves, and the Septuagint consists of translations of the different books made over a considerable period, between about the fourth and about the first centuries BC. The Greek Bible came to contain more books than the Hebrew Scriptures – all of them, however, of Jewish origin; and it was this Bible that Christians of the early centuries tended to know and to refer to. This is already true of Paul, even though he was learned in Hebrew; he wrote, and quoted the Old Testament Scriptures, in Greek.

'THE LAW AND THE PROPHETS'

The phrase, 'the law and the prophets', is the normal way of distinguishing between the Pentateuch and all other holy books in Judaism of the New Testament period, and it is reflected clearly in the Gospels (see Matt. 7:12; 11:13). 'Prophets' is a catch-all term, much wider than it would be in our own usage. As we have already seen, it covers the historical books as well as the books which *we* think of as prophetic – Isaiah, Jeremiah, and so on. In much later times these were called Latter or Later Prophets to distinguish them from the Former Prophets, i.e. what we have been calling the Deuteronomistic History (the books from Joshua to 2 Kings) – 'former' and 'latter' here meaning simply 'those that come first' and 'those that come second' in a list of biblical scrolls, and perhaps also in the way in which the scrolls were arranged in a library or book-room. But 'Prophets' also seems to have referred to other books, such as the Psalms or Job – anything, in fact, which was thought of as holy but which was not part of the Pentateuch. Thus for Judaism in New Testament times there were really two sorts of holy book: (a) the Torah, which was supreme; and (b) everything else.

A few New Testament references suggest a threefold division. Thus in Luke 24:44 we find 'the law, the prophets, and the psalms', where 'psalms' may indicate some further distinction between 'the prophets' and some other group of books, perhaps of lower status again. But on the whole, the evidence of the first century AD is that there were simply two categories of book. In the second century BC the work called Ecclesiasticus in some English Bibles (also called Sirach, or 'the Wisdom of Jesus son of Sirach'), talks of 'the law, the prophets, and the other books', but 'the other books' may well mean simply 'other books', i.e. non-scriptural books.

What is certain is that Judaism eventually came to recognise a third category, limiting 'the Prophets' to the four history books (Joshua, Judges, Samuel and Kings) and the four 'prophetic' books proper (Isaiah, Jeremiah, Ezekiel, and the Twelve shorter prophets), and placing all other non-Pentateuchal books into a category called blandly the Writings. The basis for the division seems to be mainly chronological: the Writings are the later books of the Hebrew Bible. Thus Chronicles appears there, with Ezra and Nehemiah, in a quite separate place from the early history books, and so do Psalms, Proverbs and Job, and the five scrolls read at Jewish festivals: Ruth, Ecclesiastes, the Song of Songs, Esther, and Lamentations. From a Christian perspective, it is very striking to find Daniel in the Writings, apparently no longer treated as a book of prophecy, though there is evidence that in earlier years it was regarded as prophetic in Judaism. Thus the Hebrew Bible came to be understood in such a way that it could be seen as three concentric circles, with the Torah at the centre, the Prophets (as now defined) next, and the Writings as an outside penumbra.

Christians did not see things in this way at all. For them there was only one category, 'Scripture'; and the books within it tended to be arranged by theme or type. Thus the Greek Bible, as received by Christians, began with all the historical books – Pentateuch, 'Former Prophets' (not so called), Chronicles, Ezra, Nehemiah, Esther, with two narrative books not recognised in the Hebrew Bible at all, Tobit and Judith, coming between Nehemiah and Esther (see Chapter 1). Next came the 'poetic' books – Psalms, Proverbs, Job and Ecclesiastes, and two more works not accepted in Judaism, the Wisdom of Solomon and Ecclesiasticus. Finally there were the 'prophetic books': Isaiah, Jeremiah – together with Lamentations, thought to be by Jeremiah, and the book of Baruch – Ezekiel, Daniel (which Christians regarded as prophetic), and the twelve 'minor' (i.e. shorter) prophets. There are detailed variations in the order within Christian codices, but this is the fundamental pattern.

THE BOOK OF THE TWELVE

The 12 shorter prophets (Hosea, Joel, Amos, Obadiah, Jonah, Micah, Nahum, Habakkuk, Zephaniah, Haggai, Zechariah and Malachi) are treated as a single book in the Hebrew Bible – the Book of the Twelve – and are grouped together as the 'minor prophets' in the Greek Bible. These writings come from many different periods, but there is some evidence that treating them as one has resulted in some changes and additions to the individual 'booklets'. For example, Joel and Amos – which are placed next to

each other despite perhaps 200 years having intervened
between them – share a few features in common,
including one quite lengthy oracle (Joel 2:16, Amos 1:2).
And it is sometimes suggested that Malachi was not originally a book in its own right at all, but an additional
section of the book of Zechariah which has been promoted
to the status of a separate prophet to make up the number
twelve ('Malachi' means 'my messenger', and could be
simply a title for Zechariah – though Hebrew names of
this kind do occur). The order of the Twelve is different in
the Greek Bible, but subject (as we would expect) to a
great deal of variation among the different manuscripts.

THE GOSPELS

Our four Gospels each probably began life as the authoritative account of Jesus' life and teachings in one
particular local church. Comments in early Christian
writers associate Mark, the earliest Gospel, with Rome;
and it is widely thought that Matthew took shape in
Syria, Luke in Asia Minor (in what is now Turkey), and
John in Ephesus. At this stage they probably had no
titles, though the first verse of Mark is in effect a title,
'The beginning of the news (Greek *euangelion*, "gospel")
about Jesus'. Nor were most Christians aware, probably,
that churches other than their own had different Gospels.
How, if at all, the relationship between the Gospels was
perceived in the late first and early second centuries AD is
fairly mysterious. Christian writers often quote from the
Gospels, but with little attention to which Gospel they are
quoting or, indeed, to its exact wording – quotation from
memory seems to be the norm.

But by about 150 a change has occurred. Our first clear
evidence for it is in the works of Irenaeus, Bishop of Lyons
(*c.* 130–*c.* 200). Irenaeus speaks for the first time of there

being four Gospels, and he spends some time in arguing that this is the correct – indeed, the only possible – number, for there are four winds, four points of the compass, four 'living creatures' in Revelation (4:9), and four covenants made by God with humankind. Such a forced piece of reasoning suggests that the four Gospels were already a given for Irenaeus, since the arguments would hardly convince anyone who was genuinely uncertain about how many Gospels there were. It sounds as if a 'canon' of four Gospels was already current in his day, at least in the Greek-speaking churches in the south of France. Not long after this, the Christian philosopher Clement (*c.* 150–*c.* 215), who taught in Alexandria in Egypt, compared John with the other three Gospels, saying that the others (the Synoptics) were earthly but John was a 'spiritual' Gospel. This again implies that, for him, the four Gospels we now have were a given. Many other Gospels were known in the early Church, but none of them is likely to be earlier than the four now accepted, with the possible exception of a few fragments in the Gospel of Thomas, which was discovered in Egypt in 1945–6, and is simply a collection of (alleged) sayings of Jesus, with no narrative framework.

Thus the four Gospels had been collected by some point in the second century AD. This is not to say that every church would have possessed all four. It only means that all four were regarded with esteem, even by churches that might not know them for themselves. The process of collection, however, made it necessary to distinguish them from each other by name. So far as we can tell from the earliest manuscripts, this was done by attaching the labels 'According to Mark', 'According to John', and so on. The word 'Gospel' itself does not appear in the titles, and does not seem at this stage to have been a generic title for a particular kind of book. Mark is simply 'the good news as recounted by Mark'. Justin Martyr (*c*. 100–*c*. 165) seems almost deliberately to avoid calling the individual books 'Gospels', which might have seemed to imply that there was more than one 'good news'. This avoidance, however, suggests that some people already did use the word in that sense. And Irenaeus talks about 'the Gospels' quite unconcernedly. So our present usage was not long in establishing itself.

The order of the four Gospels – we can speak literally of order, because the Christians very soon began to use the codex for their Scriptures – did not become constant until well into the Christian era. Irenaeus lists them in several different orders, none of them identical to ours. Various criteria may have operated: for example, Matthew and John might have come first on the grounds that they were written by apostles, Mark and Luke next because those who wrote them were only *apostolici*, disciples of the apostles. (Mark is supposed to have recorded what Peter told him, Luke to have been the companion of Paul: neither, therefore, was an eye-witness.) Modern biblical scholars do not think that any of the Gospels is by an apostle, but everyone in antiquity thought that Matthew and John were. Alternatively, they might have been listed in supposed order of composition. Eusebius of Caesarea (*c*. 260–*c*. 340), the first historian of the Christian Church, lists them in the order with which we are now familiar – Matthew, Mark, Luke, John – on chronological grounds.

THE PAULINE LETTERS

A collection of Paul's epistles seems to go back as far as a collection of the Gospels, into the second or third generation after the apostle himself. Once again, the order varies – but in general, the length of the epistles seems to be a prime consideration. The epistles to churches seem regularly to have been in the order we know now: Romans, 1 and 2 Corinthians, Galatians, Ephesians, Philippians, Colossians, 1 and 2 Thessalonians; though where Hebrews was thought to be Pauline, it tended to be included after Romans in the list (again on grounds of length). Then come the letters to individuals: 1 and 2 Timothy, Titus and Philemon. Arrangement by length may have reversed the chronological order as far as the two Corinthian and two Thessalonian letters are concerned – nothing in the text itself tells us which is the first letter in each case, and 2 Corinthians implies that Paul wrote several letters to Corinth. It is slightly odd that Galatians always precedes Ephesians, which is actually longer. One hypothesis is that there was once a collection beginning with Ephesians, to which Romans, Corinthians and Galatians were then added. Perhaps, as some have suggested, the first Pauline collection was made by Onesimus, the slave mentioned in Philemon, who seems to have become an 'overseer' (which approximately means a bishop) in a Pauline church.

We might wonder as to the motive for collecting Paul's letters, which deal with such local and specific issues in many cases – Philemon being the limiting case of this. A stray reference in Colossians (which may not be genuinely Pauline, however) suggests that Paul intended his letters to be read in more than one congregation: 'When this letter has been read among you, have it read also in the church of the Laodiceans; and see that you read also the letter from Laodicea' (Col. 4:16). Generalising this principle could have led the Church to turn all Paul's letters into a composite document, perceived to be of general interest to Christians.

THE REST OF THE NEW TESTAMENT

In our printed Bibles, John's Gospel is followed by the
Acts of the Apostles, then by Paul's epistles, and then by
what are sometimes called the catholic (meaning general
or universal) epistles: James, 1 and 2 Peter, 1, 2 and 3
John, and Jude. Strangely, this is not the order which was
common in the Church of the first few centuries, where
Acts stood at the head, not of the Pauline corpus, but of
the catholic epistles. If Gospels and Pauline epistles
formed two collections, then Acts and the catholic epistles
formed a third. The Christian New Testament was thus
coincidentally not unlike the Hebrew Bible in having
three principal sections which sometimes appeared as
three separate codices – though Revelation spoils the
symmetry by standing alone as a fourth section in some
manuscripts.

Acts is a particularly interesting case of how the
arrangement of the Bible has disrupted what we assume
to have been the original intentions of the writers. Acts is
volume 2 of a work which has Luke's Gospel as volume 1,
as the prologue (Acts 1:1) makes clear. But there is to my
knowledge no manuscript in which the two books appear
side by side. Acts is always regarded as coming in the
third category, with the non-Pauline letters. One effect of
this was that early Christian writers cited it much less
often than Luke. For reading in church, Luke, as a Gospel,
was far more important than Acts.

The order of the catholic epistles is again determined by
their length, except that, naturally enough, the Petrine
and Johannine letters are kept together, though in order
of length within each set.

WHO COLLECTED THE SCRIPTURES?

We asked in the last chapter: Who wrote the books? Now we have to ask: Who collected them? This second question has no simpler an answer than the first. The collection and dissemination of the Jewish and Christian Scriptures was an infinitely complicated and varied process.

We have a fairly good idea of why the Torah, the five books of Moses, came to be gathered together and treated as in some sense a single work ('the five-fifths of the law'). We can read off the motive from the fact that 'Torah' is what these books came to be called. Despite their clear narrative character and the miscellaneous material they contain, the books of the Pentateuch were experienced by later generations first and foremost as instruction in how to live a good Jewish life. It is therefore likely that they were gathered together by people who were entrusted with the regulation of Jewish life, something like what we would now call rabbis, or perhaps lawyers. A secondary but very important motive for collecting the books of the Torah was so that they could be solemnly read in the liturgy – secondary because the reason for so reading them was their already central role as moral instruction, but important because it determined the form that these books would have from then on, as scrolls produced with loving care and an enormous concern for accuracy.

The other books do not have the same central function in Judaism, and we can only guess at how they came to be gathered together into collections, eventually settling into the twofold division of Prophets and Writings. This distinction, which seems to have arrived on the scene some time later than the writing of the New Testament (which is unaware of it), may be connected with liturgical use of the non-Torah books. The rule in the synagogue today, which goes back well into antiquity, is that after the weekly reading from the Pentateuch, a second reading is added. This second reading has to come from the Prophets, not from the Writings. But the second readings (*haftarot*) have in practice been fixed for a very long time, and it is possible that the rule is reflected in the division of the Scriptures, rather than the other way round – in other words, that the Prophets are those books which contributed *haftarot* to the lectionary, and the Writings those that did not. It is also true that the Writings tends to contain later works than the Prophets, though not universally so (e.g. Zechariah, in the Prophets, is probably later in its date of composition than Psalms, in the Writings). But it is fairly doubtful whether Jews at the beginning of our era *knew* which books were older than which. The only safe conclusion is that we simply do not know how these two collections came to be put together.

Equally mysterious is the compilation of the Gospels. If it is true that originally each Gospel belonged to a particular church and was its local version of the Good News, then the shift to recognising four different and often inconsistent witnesses to the gospel must have been a major, and perhaps traumatic, change of attitude. As we shall see later, the acceptance of four inconsistent accounts means that none of them can any longer be considered absolutely authoritative: each has the power to modify the story told by the others.

There was certainly resistance to the promulgation of a four-Gospel collection. We can see this in the work of Marcion (died *c.* 160), who insisted that there was only one true Gospel, Luke – and that only once he had expurgated it, so that it supported his own style of Christianity. It is clear from this that other Gospels must have been circulating, and we know that Marcion's contemporary, Justin Martyr, quoted from all three Synoptics though not from John, and did not raise any question about their mutual compatibility. This suggests that the Gospels – or at least the Synoptics – were already widely seen as a coherent set of documents in the early second century AD. This seems to have come about without much controversy, which is remarkable when one stops to think how odd it is that the Church should have four alternative versions of the events and teachings which it regards as utterly crucial! Though Marcion's opposition to this state of affairs died away among his successors, some early Christian writers did think that a single, homogenised Gospel would be better than four inconsistent ones. The most famous example of this movement is in the work of Tatian. In about 150–60 he produced the *Diatessaron*, a Gospel-harmony, which was a great success in some of the Eastern churches, and continued to be used by many Christians even after all had come to recognise the four-Gospel collection as authoritative. Gospel-harmonies – single accounts, ironing out all inconsistencies and amalgamating all the stories / teachings in one book – continue to this day to be used by some Christians.

If Paul's admonition to the Colossians to read his letter to the Laodiceans (and vice versa) is authentic, we may see the collection of his epistles as going back to an impulse deriving from Paul himself. Some scholars have even spoken of Paul 'publishing' his letters – making copies of a number of them and having them circulated to all the churches he had founded. If this did not happen in Paul's lifetime, it is fairly likely to have happened soon afterwards: the production of deutero-Pauline letters such as the Pastorals implies that people would read and value letters purporting to be by Paul. Marcion, again, had a Pauline letter-collection, and it seems unlikely that he was the first to think of this, since he omitted sections of the letters of which he disapproved, presumably implying that he (and those who condemned him for his vandalism) already knew the letters in their fuller form. Of course we cannot say how far the 'Pauline corpus' was thought of as a single work, and how far the differences between the various epistles were seen and noted. The best we can say is that the letters formed a collection in a more than simply accidental sense – as though they merely happened all to exist in the same room – yet in less than the way they appear to us, who can go into any book shop and buy a book containing exactly the same letters in the same order. Collections of books in the ancient world were more varied, less consistent, than they are for us.

CHAPTER FOUR

From Books to Scriptures

WHAT IS SCRIPTURE?

One way of thinking about the Bible is to see it as given by God, at one moment or at many moments, to two communities: ancient Israel and the early Church. On this model the books that now form the Bible have always been the Scriptures – the inspired, holy writings – of God's people. The title of this chapter, 'From books to Scriptures', is then more or less meaningless.

But an alternative model, the one I have been using, sees the books that form the Bible as having arisen in a wide range of human contexts and at various times, often as the result of the work of many hands. A moment of revelation cannot be identified. If we are to speak of God giving the Scriptures to people, it can only be in and through this human process. The implication is that the books did not all begin life as 'Scripture', but came to be received as such through a process, which may have been long or short. To begin with they were simply books.

Special from the start

While it is important to recognise that the contents of Scripture started life as simply books, it should not lead to exaggeration. First, there are books in both Testaments that seem deliberately designed to have an official status. Deuteronomy, for example, presents itself as the last words addressed by Moses to the tribes of Israel in the plains of Moab, across the Jordan, immediately before his death. This cannot have been intended as a casual, interesting book with no particular authority. It must have been designed from the beginning to have the status that came to belong to Scripture in Judaism and Christianity. Deuteronomy is a self-consciously scriptural book. The point can be grasped all the more easily if we compare it with one or two Old Testament books which are more likely to have been designed for some other purpose. For example, most scholars think that the Song of Songs originated as a set of erotic poems of very high quality, which were only later treated as scriptural: this was achieved by regarding the lovers in the poems as representative, allegorically, of God and Israel (Jesus and the Church, in the Christian version of the allegory). Or again, Proverbs mostly presents itself as the wise sayings of a human teacher, rather than of God: to treat it as divine revelation is surely to reinterpret its original intention.

In the New Testament, it is equally easy to argue that a number of books began life as human documents. Paul's epistles are obviously the apostle's comments and instructions, arising from the particular situation of the churches to which he was writing. In the case of Philemon, the situation is extremely particular and special. It would be odd to say that Philemon began life as a piece of Scripture, even though (as we shall see) it succeeded perfectly well in becoming one. On the other hand, John's Gospel (unlike the Synoptics) seems to make scriptural claims for itself. This can be seen especially in the opening words – 'In the beginning was the Word' – which immediately invite comparison with Genesis 1:1, and suggest that John is a kind of Christian equivalent of Genesis. At the very least, John seems to be designed as a solemn and careful exposition of the life of Jesus from a highly individual standpoint; it is clearly as far as possible from being simply a set of anecdotes! So here too we may say that some kind of scriptural status was implicit from the start.

A special selection

A second factor is this. If the books of the Old and New Testaments were all the literature that ever existed in Israel and in the early Church, it might be reasonable to expect that secular and sacred books would both be represented in Scripture. After all, it would be surprising to find a nation whose writings were only ever about sacred subjects – though where the Church is concerned this might be more plausible, since the Church was a religious movement, not a nation. But it seems clear that in both cases there were more books in existence than came in time to form the Bible. The Church had many more documents than those which form the Bible, many of which have been discovered in modern times – for example, documents excavated at Nag Hammadi in Egypt, such as the Gospel of Thomas, mentioned in Chapter 3. Where ancient Israel is concerned, the Old Testament itself mentions many books which have now perished, such as the 'book of Jashar' (2 Sam. 1:18) and the chronicles of the kings of Israel and Judah (see 2 Kings 15:26 and 16:19). The books in the Old and New Testaments are those which came to be accepted as 'holy', in some sense; they were not just all the books which happened to exist. As we shall see in Chapter 5, that does not necessarily mean that someone consciously selected them from a longer list of possibilities. Most of them seem to have been accepted from the beginning. But they were books recognised widely as of high quality: reckoning them to be Scripture was not a matter of taking just any books which might have been lying around and deciding to call them 'The Holy Bible'.

So the suggestion that the books we have been discussing 'became' Scripture contains an important truth, but should not lead us to think that it was simply an open question which books would achieve this status. Some had been written with a high status in mind from the beginning. Both the Pentateuch and the prophetic books make a claim inside the text itself to have been divinely inspired, and the Gospel of John, at least, seems designed to be a kind of Christian Scripture.

We have been bandying the word 'Scripture' around for many pages now, but have never defined it. In this chapter I intend to ask what is implied in calling a book 'scriptural', and how such books were read in the ancient world. A good working definition of Scripture is that of S. Z. Leiman: '[Books] accepted by Jews as authoritative for religious practice and/or doctrine, and whose authority is binding upon the Jewish people for all generations'.* (The same formula, obviously, could be adapted to apply to Christian Scripture.) To unpack what this implies, I shall outline a number of ways in which the reading of such books tended to differ from the way in which ordinary books would have been read. When some or all of these features are present, we can reasonably say that a given book is regarded as scriptural.

1　CITATIONS

One way of telling that a book is regarded as scriptural is to observe the way in which other books refer to it. The New Testament writers frequently quote the Old Testa-

---

* S. Z. Leiman, *The Canonization of Hebrew Scripture: The Talmudic and Midrashic Evidence*, Hamden, Conn. 1976, p. 14.

ment, often with formulas such as 'as it is written', or 'the Scripture says' (see Rom. 3:10; 11:8; Gal. 4:30). Early Christian writers cite New Testament books with similar formulas, making it clear that they regarded these as having the same, or a similar, scriptural status. Thus a scriptural book is one that can be cited as an authority for this or that point; once the quotation has been mentioned, the argument is clinched.

On this basis it can be said with certainty that almost all the books in the present Old Testament were regarded as scriptural by the beginning of the Christian era if not sooner, and that almost all the books of the New Testament were scriptural for most Christians by about the third century AD. We must not base conclusions on an absence of evidence: the fact that, for example, the New Testament does not quote Esther, or that a second-century writer such as Justin Martyr does not quote John, cannot be made to prove that these books were not scriptural for the people in question, only that we do not know whether they were or not. Just as there are a few books whose scriptural status is not firmly attested, so there are also books now not biblical which are sometimes cited on an equal footing with those that are. Notoriously, the epistle of Jude (14–15) cites the First Book of Enoch, which now survives only in the Ethiopic languages, apparently regarding it as scriptural – it is treated as an inspired prophecy. If this is felt to be a citation of one rather marginal book by another, it can be pointed out that both Paul and Hebrews seem happy to draw on the Wisdom of Solomon, which was never in the Hebrew Scriptures (unlike some other apocryphal works, it was written in Greek, not translated from Hebrew). Wisdom continued to be a most important book in the Christian Church, and there seems no reason to doubt that Paul regarded it as Scripture. One of Jesus' own sayings in the Gospels seems to draw on Ecclesiasticus, admittedly without a citation formula. (See Matt. 11:28–9 and Ecclus. 51:26–7.) Thus a list of the books that were scriptural in New Testament times would not exactly coincide with the present Old Testament. But the area of agreement is enormous: more than 90 per cent of the Old Testament was undisputed, while on the other hand, only a few other works seem to have been given anything approaching equal credence.

A fascinating phenomenon, related to the very long time over which the Bible was formed, is the quotation of one biblical book by another. In the case of New Testament citations of the Old Testament, this is not surprising – but 'inner-testamental' quotation initially seems unexpected. The second letter of Peter, one of the latest books in the New Testament, talks about Paul's epistles as though, for the author, they were already Scripture: 'There are some things in them hard to understand, which the ignorant and unstable twist to their own destruction, as they do the other Scriptures' (2 Pet. 3:16). In the Old Testament, Deuteronomy 24:16 ('The fathers shall not be put to death for the children, nor shall the children be put to death for the fathers') is cited in both 2 Kings 14:6 and Ezekiel 18:20; 1 Kings 22:28 cites the opening words of the book of Micah, 'Hear, all you people' (Mic. 1:2 – apparently thinking that Micaiah, son of Imlah, is the same person as Micah of Moresheth).

2 AUTHORSHIP

A second feature of scriptural books is their authorship. In principle, every scriptural book is thought to have been written by a person important in the history of salvation. In New Testament times it was widely assumed that every scriptural book was written by a prophet. Thus the

Jewish writer Josephus, writing late in the first century AD, says that all Scriptures were written before the time of Artaxerxes (probably meaning the Persian king contemporary with Ezra, in the late fifth century). After that, books on the history of the Jews had continued to be written, but had 'not been deemed worthy of equal credit with the earlier records, because of the failure of the exact succession of the prophets'. David and Solomon were also seen as prophets in this period (hence Psalms and Proverbs are both Scripture), and Moses, after all, was the prophet *par excellence*.

Where the New Testament is concerned, many Christians believed that, to be scriptural, a book must have been written by an apostle or, at least, someone who had known the apostles. Matthew and John were assumed to be by the apostles of those names, Mark and Luke by friends of Peter and Paul respectively. All the catholic epistles claim apostles as their authors: James, Peter, John, and Jude (that is, Judas, the one who was not Judas Iscariot).

There are two points to be made about this, one obvious and the other rather less so. The more obvious point is that those who read the Old or New Testament at about the end of the first century AD did not have any evidence with which to decide whether claims such as these were true or not. Even for us, after several centuries of detailed textual study, it is not possible to say with certainty whether 1 and 2 Timothy, say, which claim to be by Paul, are genuine or not, though there is a broad consensus that they probably aren't. Occasionally, writers in antiquity were able to notice suspicious features: Origen (c. 185–c. 254), for example, argued that Hebrews was not by Paul because the literary style was different from his. But Origen was an exceptional scholar. For the most part, writers in this period were quite unable to know whether or not the authorship claimed for ancient books was true or false.

But the second point is this. Ascribing authority to a book because of the writer's identity can work in two directions. People may come across a book which claims to be by an apostle, and consequently they may take it very seriously. On the other hand, they may read a book of unknown authorship, and may feel that it is so good that it must have been written by an apostle. The same process can also work negatively. A book may seem so bad that no one is prepared to believe its claim to be by an apostle; or alternatively, because a book does not claim to be by an apostle, people may not take it seriously, and will assume that its contents are not very important. To put it another way, if people like a book and it also claims apostolic authorship, the two features bolster each other up. If they do not like it, they will not believe the attribution to an apostle; if it is not attributed to an apostle, they may not like it. The point is quite familiar to us in other spheres: the news that a painting is a fake leads us to expect less of it; a painting which strikes us as poor will lead us to think it may be a fake.

We have to say, therefore, that supposed prophetic/ apostolic authorship went hand-in-hand with scriptural status for books in Judaism and early Christianity. But deciding whether the authorship conveyed the status, or the perceived status resulted in conclusions about authorship, is often an impossible task. We do know that many works believed by Jews and Christians to be holy – both from within and from outside what is now the Bible – are pseudonymous: for example, Proverbs in the Old Testament and Enoch outside it; 2 Peter in the New Testament, and the Epistle of the Apostles (*c.* 150) outside it. But it has to be discovered in each case (and sometimes cannot be discovered at all) whether the pseudonymous attribution is the cause or the result of the status such books were felt to have.

3 DATE

Similar considerations apply to the date of scriptural works as to their authorship. Indeed, date and authorship go together. If all the New Testament writings are supposed to be by apostles or disciples of apostles, that implies that they must have been written within a generation or so of the death of Jesus. (In fact, as we have seen, some are almost certainly a good bit later than this.) Similarly, if all the Hebrew Scriptures were written by prophets, and prophecy ceased to occur after the time of Ezra, then they must have been complete before about the end of the fifth century BC.

However, our second point about authorship applies here as well. If there is a chronological cut-off point for the writing of scriptural books, then certainly any book known to be later will not count as Scripture. In Judaism this does seem to have been the criterion which led to Ecclesiasticus being regarded as non-scriptural, even though it was held in high esteem: the prologue to the book itself indicates that it was written in the second century BC. But conversely, any book that people feel disposed to reject on other grounds will tend to be written off as 'late'.

The case of Daniel is interesting here. On the face of it, Daniel was written during the Exile, in the sixth century BC: Daniel was a contemporary of Ezekiel, according to the book itself. Josephus accepted this at face value, and consequently the fact that Daniel is a scriptural book does not come into conflict with his principle that all the Scriptures were written before the death of Artaxerxes. In the present arrangement of the Hebrew Bible, however,

Daniel appears not in the Prophets section but among the Writings, and this may preserve an awareness that the book was in reality from the second century BC, the age of the Maccabean martyrs, as most scholars now think.

If there was an end-point for the writing of Scripture, there was also, for some, a starting-point, in the work of Moses. Many writings between about 200 BC and AD 200 seek, as it were, to trump Moses, by purporting to come from earlier figures. Enoch was felt to be a fairly safe bet, having lived only a few generations after Adam – and there are even books attributed to Adam and Eve. Only a book by an angel could be earlier than that! It may be that the eventual non-acceptance of such works into the Scriptures reflects an application of the rule that no Scripture was written before Moses, any more than for Josephus any was written after Ezra. On the other hand, many of these pseudonymous works were treated seriously by writers in the New Testament period, and Enoch, as we saw above, is cited in the New Testament as a prophecy.

4   RELEVANCE TO PRESENT CONCERNS

Anyone who has attended a Christian Bible-study knows that there are certain things which cannot properly be said in such a context. Chief among these is any suggestion that the text being read has no relevance to our concerns and has, in fact, nothing to say to us. This is because Christians believe that the Bible is always relevant in all possible circumstances, and that it will always illuminate their lives if they read it properly. One major implication of calling a book scriptural or biblical is this contemporary applicability.

We can see easily that this is how the New Testament writers read the Old Testament. Indeed, they often went beyond thinking of Scripture as generally relevant, and claimed that it was very specifically relevant to the concerns of the early Church. Paul says of the disobedience of the Israelites in the wilderness, 'Now these things happened to them as a warning, but they were written down for our instruction, upon whom the end of the ages has come' (1 Cor. 10:11); or again, citing Isaiah 49:8, ' "At the acceptable time I have listened to you, and helped you on the day of salvation." Behold, now is the acceptable time; behold, now is the day of salvation' (2 Cor. 6:2).

In some forms of Judaism there was much the same sense that the old Scriptures had been foretelling a great event which was now coming about – the community that produced the Dead Sea Scrolls believed this, and quoted texts from the prophets which it believed had predicted its own history. But in the type of Judaism that came to be called 'rabbinic' – and in due course became the norm – it is more common to find scriptural texts read for their *universal* applicability and relevance. For example, in the Mishnah – a compilation of rabbinic teachings and rulings made in the second century AD – biblical texts are usually cited to ground ethical rules. Interestingly enough, alongside the Pentateuch, the book of Proverbs provides the bulk of the texts quoted by rabbinic authors, who saw it as a compendium of always relevant texts.

5 UNIVERSALITY

If Scripture is relevant at all times, it is also relevant to all people. This means that some way needed to be found of reducing the particularity of the biblical texts. The classic New Testament example of this is Paul's epistle to Philemon, which concerns one extremely local and specific case – a runaway slave who has gone to Paul for protection, and whom Paul is returning to his owner with an exhortation to clemency. In point of fact, it is far from hard to extract a general 'message' from this letter, for Paul himself appeals to general Christian principles in urging Philemon not to punish Onesimus. But we might say that if we were *designing* a scriptural book, we would hardly produce Philemon. At all events, the early Church found a very effective way of generalising this and every other one of Paul's epistles, by collecting them into the Pauline corpus which could then be treated as a source of doctrine and instruction in every generation – as continues to be the case.

In the Muratorian Fragment – a list of the biblical books probably from the fourth century (which we shall look at in Chapter 5) – a parallel is drawn between Paul's letters to seven churches (Rome, Corinth, Galatia, Ephesus, Philippi, Colossae, and Thessalonica) and the book of Revelation, which is John's letter 'to the seven churches' (different churches, but the similarity is striking: see Rev. 1:4). The author of the Fragment then says that Paul wrote to seven churches just as John did: 'The blessed apostle Paul himself, following the example of his predecessor John, wrote only to seven churches by name ... yet it is evident that one church is spread throughout the whole world. For John also, although in the Apocalypse he wrote to seven churches, nevertheless speaks to all.' Similarly Tertullian (*c.* 160–*c.* 225) says that it does not matter if Colossians is called Laodiceans, because Paul was not writing specifically to one church but with all Christians in mind: 'The titles do not matter, since in writing to any particular people the apostle was writing to all.' This seems to be a universal effect of treating a book as Scripture: it is loosened from its specific situation, and comes to be seen as belonging to all times and all places.

6 MUTUAL CONSISTENCY

As soon as there is a collection of biblical books, they will tend to be read in ways that enable them to be perceived as consistent with each other. One of the clearest cases of this is the four Gospels. Each of the Gospels inherently makes a claim to be *the* truth about what Jesus did and taught and suffered: Luke explicitly says that he has compared other existing accounts and is now presenting the definitive version (see Luke 1:1–4). Matthew represents a clear upgrading of Mark, making available a fuller and more 'correct' account of Jesus' life. This kind of activity did not cease in the Church with the last of the four evangelists, but was continued by two or three subsequent writers. As discussed in Chapter 3 above, Marcion took Luke's Gospel, which was apparently the one he was most familiar with in his own church in Pontus, and 'corrected' it to remove all quotations of the Old Testament Scriptures and any suggestions that Jesus was the son of the creator-god worshipped by the Jews, thus bringing it into line with his own unorthodox system of thought. In the next generation Tatian took the four Gospels and made a single version out of them by harmonising all the inconsistencies: his *Diatessaron* enjoyed a great success in the Syrian churches until the fifth century, and was still used by some through the Middle Ages and into modern times. Justin Martyr seems to have used his own digest of the three Synoptic Gospels, rather than the three as separate books. In all these ways a desire to revise the Gospels and produce one definitive version can be seen to have lived on in the Church after the evangelists themselves.

But the view that eventually prevailed in the Church is the one espoused by Irenaeus, described in Chapter 3: that there are four Gospels, and that all of them are necessary just as they stand. Once this was accepted, each of the Gospels had a modifying effect on how the others were read. Since there cannot be any incompatibilities between four perfectly true documents, apparent discrepancies have to be reinterpreted. Clement of Alexandria suggested that John differed from the Synoptics because it was a 'spiritual' Gospel, whatever precisely that means. John highlighted events with a spiritual significance, and so it is not surprising if he left out many of the stories found in the Synoptics. Anyway, he knew the other three and was assuming that his readers would too: he was taking them for granted. Another useful suggestion, made by Eusebius, was that the events in the opening chapters of John took place before John the Baptist was imprisoned, i.e. before the first events recorded in Mark. In practice this makes nonsense of both John and the Synoptics, but it does superficially make the discrepancies seem less urgent. As we saw in the previous chapter, Christian writers came to see each Gospel as 'the good news, according to Mark/Matthew/Luke/John', rather than as the unique, correct version of the gospel message.

When two books on the same subject are both regarded as scriptural, readers will adjust their approach in order to make the books compatible and consistent in this way. There are similar records of rabbinic problems with inconsistencies in the Hebrew Scriptures. The book of Ezekiel gave the rabbis problems because its laws about the rights and duties of the priests (Ezek. 44) cannot be reconciled with the legislation on this subject in the Torah (e.g. Num. 3). A certain Hananiah, son of Hezekiah, is said to have used up 300 barrels of oil keeping his lamp burning at night until he had succeeded in reconciling the discrepancies. Strangely, there seems to have been no awareness among the rabbis of the major discrepancies in the biblical narrative books, for example between Kings and Chronicles or between the different sources in Genesis or Exodus – at least, these things are never discussed in the rabbinic literature that has come down to us. One likely explanation is that they were concerned only for discrepancies in the *law*, where a reconciliation had to be found before Jewish practice could be properly regulated. Historical discrepancies did not matter much, because nothing followed from the historical books about Jewish practice. On the other hand, Christians went to their special Scriptures, the New Testament, for information about what Jesus had done and taught, and for that inconsistent narratives were a problem.

7 EXCESS OF MEANING

Another feature of holy books in the ancient world is that people tended to interpret them as more full of meaning than ordinary texts. In a way, this is already implicit in the acceptance of their universal applicability and complete consistency among themselves, for ordinary texts are not like that. But what I have in mind here is a meaning which is much more profound and far-reaching than the surface of the text would lead one to expect. Both Jewish and Christian commentators see discrepancies and inconsistencies as intended by God to point to deeper truths. Far from being a problem, they are signals of just how profound the text really is.

This is one way of seeing some of the New Testament's interpretation of 'messianic' texts in the Old Testament. In Acts 2:22–36, for example, Peter examines the text from Psalm 16, 'Thou wilt not abandon my soul to Hades, nor let thy Holy One see corruption.' He argues that this text is puzzling, taken at face value, because David (assumed to be the speaker) did die, and his body corrupted in the grave. But the puzzle is solved if David were referring to the coming King, the Messiah. Jesus is this Messiah, and the resurrection proves that his body did not corrupt. So if we read the text in the light of what we know of Jesus, Peter says, we find that it is no longer a problem. It simply contained a much greater weight of meaning than anyone had suspected.

Jewish interpreters worked with the same logic when confronted with problem texts. The Jewish scholar Philo (20 BC–AD 50), working in Alexandria, was faced with a puzzle, in the Greek version of the Scriptures which he used, in Psalm 74 (75 in the Hebrew). The Psalm says, 'In the hand of the Lord there is a cup of unmixed wine full of mixture' – an obvious self-contradiction. Philo comments as follows: 'The powers which God employs are unmixed in respect of himself, but mixed to created beings. For it cannot be that mortal nature should have room for the unmixed. We cannot look even upon the sun's flame untempered.' The comment is a long way from the natural meaning of the Psalm, but it shows very clearly how an interpreter can take a problem in a text and show that in reality it enshrines a deeper truth. No one interprets everyday texts in this way; it is a mark of scriptural status.

One sign of the New Testament's status for Christians is that it, too, came to be subjected to this kind of interpretation. Often the method used was allegorisation – taking the obvious meaning of the text to refer to something quite different. One of the most famous examples of this is Augustine's interpretation of the parable of the Good Samaritan. For him the Samaritan is to be understood as a symbol of Christ, and what the Samaritan does literally for the wounded man is what Christ does for us, metaphorically:

A certain man went down from Jerusalem to Jericho;

Adam himself is meant; *Jerusalem* is the heavenly city of peace, from whose blessedness Adam fell; *Jericho* means the moon, and signifies our mortality, because it is born, waxes, wanes, and dies. *Thieves* are the devil and his angels. *Who stripped him*, namely, of his immortality; *and beat him*, by persuading him to sin; *and left him half dead*, because in so far as man can understand and know God, he lives, but in so far as he is wasted and oppressed by sin, he is dead; he is therefore called *half dead*. *The priest and Levite* who saw him and passed by, signify the priesthood and ministry of the *Old Testament*, which could profit nothing for salvation. *Samaritan* means Guardian, and therefore the Lord himself is signified by this name. The *binding* of the wounds is the restraint of sin. *Oil* is the comfort of good hope; *wine* the exhortation to work with fervent spirit. The *beast* is the flesh in which he deigned to come to us. The being *set upon the beast* is belief in the incarnation of Christ. The *inn* is the Church, where travellers returning to their heavenly country are refreshed after pilgrimage. The *morrow* is after the resurrection of the Lord. The *two pence* are either the two precepts of love, or the promise of this life and of that which is to come. The *innkeeper* is the Apostle [Paul]. The supererogatory payment is either his counsel of celibacy, or the fact that he worked with his hands lest he should be a burden to any of the weaker brethren when the gospel was new, though it was lawful to him 'to live by the gospel'.

Augustine, *Quaestiones Evangeliorum* 2:19

It is fair to say that anyone who reads a text allegorically regards it as extremely important: only texts with high prestige are read in such a way. Thus, somewhat paradoxically, proposing a forced and unnatural meaning for a text is usually a tribute to its status! In the ancient world in general – not just in Judaism and Christianity – allegorical reading was practised only on 'classic' texts, the books of Homer being the most important example. Origen tells us that his opponent, Celsus, objected that Christian texts (by which he meant both Testaments) were full of inconsistencies. Origen's response is not to deny the inconsistencies, but to tell Celsus that he must be very stupid if he cannot see that the Bible is meant to be read allegorically. In its time, this was a potentially convincing rejoinder.

8   HOLY BOOKS AS SACRED OBJECTS

Finally, a feature which seems to occur all over the world is a tendency to treat as holy the actual physical books containing holy texts, and to handle them with signs of reverence. Christians eventually developed such practices with their Bible, and especially with the Gospels. In Western Catholic and Eastern Orthodox liturgy, Gospelbooks are often specially ornate, often carried in procession and honoured with incense and kisses. Carrying a Bible into church in a solemn way is often a feature of Protestant worship too. But in the first couple of centuries there is not much evidence of such customs. On the contrary, early New Testament manuscripts tend to be written in rather informal handwriting, and the use of the codex, universal for Christian Bibles, was originally a mark of casual writing, not of a holy book. But in Judaism there is a clear correlation between the holiness of the Scriptures and the form in which they are written, and Jews developed elaborate rules about how biblical texts should and should not be written.

One particular concern in all Jewish texts is the correct writing of the name of God, which consists of the four consonants YHWH. This may well originally have been pronounced 'Yahweh'; but by the New Testament period no one ever did pronounce it, because it was too holy. Texts which contained the name were regarded as participating in the holiness of the name of God himself, and hence had to be handled with particular reverence, stored properly, and when worn out buried with solemnity. Some early Christians wrote the name of God in Hebrew characters in their own (otherwise Greek) documents, and this posed a problem for Jews. Christian books were, obviously, not holy to Jews, but if God's name appeared in them, they seemed to call for reverence. So rabbis ruled that heretical books like those of the Christians might be destroyed 'with their names'. The controversy reminds us, however, that whether or not a book is treated with reverence may depend less on its content than on its physical appearance – especially, of course, for someone who is illiterate and cannot read the book anyway. There is a sense in which a book was holy in Judaism if it looked like a Torah scroll, and especially if it contained special signs – those indicating the divine name. We are not speaking here at the formal, scholarly level of a rabbi, but guessing at what may have been the case for the average illiterate or semiliterate worshipper, for whom books were a bit of a mystery anyway.

FROM BOOKS TO SCRIPTURE

In all these ways the books of the Old and New Testaments were regarded as 'Scripture' by the end of the second century AD at the latest. Most of them had been so regarded for much longer than that. The category 'sacred book' was a familiar one in the ancient world, even outside Judaism and Christianity, and there is no doubt that the Scriptures of Jews and Christians fitted into it well. There is, however, one feature about the Christians' attitude to the Gospels which needs to be mentioned here, since it suggests that at the beginnings of the Christian movement they did not fit this category as well as they would later come to do.

The earliest understanding of the Gospels seems to have been that they were important historical records, rather than Scriptures akin to those of the Old Testament. Marcion would not have felt free to revise Luke, or for that matter Luke have felt free to revise Mark, if these books had been seen as holy Scriptures. Christian use of the codex was originally a quite natural way of recording what were seen not as books, in the technical sense, but as jottings or drafts. There was a strong feeling in the early Church that written texts were not the best means of transmitting the gospel, which was in essence an oral proclamation; the Gospels were widely perceived as collections of the raw material from which such a proclamation could be composed, not as finished products in their own right. Whether this is how the Gospel *writers* themselves saw the matter is doubtful – indeed, modern biblical criticism has shown that the Gospels are far more sophisticated literary works than such an interpretation implies. But it is certainly how many in the first generation or two of Gospel *readers* saw it. Such an understanding did not last, probably could not last, in a world where holy books were a normal part of religion: it was more or less inevitable that Christian books would be assimilated to the model of 'Scripture'. But it is worth remembering that there was a time when the Gospels were supremely important, yet were not thought of as Scripture, and consequently not subject to many of the kinds of interpretation we have been surveying in this chapter.

CHAPTER FIVE

Fixing the Canon

It is important to see that the three processes we have studied so far are logically distinct. Writing books is not the same as collecting them, and neither writing nor collecting is the same as starting to treat them as Scripture. But it is equally important to see that they are not three distinct historical phases in the development of the Bible, as though for some centuries people were writing books, for a few more other people were collecting them, and then for a few more again they all came to be treated as Scripture. The three processes overlap. Deuteronomy and, probably, John's Gospel, were making an implicit claim to be Scripture right from the beginning. Some books had already come to be seen as Scripture before others, which are now in the Bible, had even been written. Thus the Pentateuch was probably already collected and regarded as holy before some of the later prophets had even been born. By the time Daniel and Ecclesiastes were written, Judaism already had a 'Bible'. Similarly with the New Testament. Paul's epistles had probably already been collected into a corpus before the writing of 2 Peter, which refers to them as if they were already a familiar work. The Bible grew in a most untidy way, and no amount of wishful thinking will make it otherwise.

There was a fourth process to be completed before the Bible came to exist in exactly the form in which we have it. People sometimes talk of the 'canon' of Scripture, and of the process that gave us the Bible as its 'canonisation'. I have avoided the term until now, but must now explain why. 'Canonisation', when used of biblical texts, tends to

mean either of two things – or both things, regarded confusingly as though they were not distinct. One is the
process described in Chapter 3: the stages by which
certain texts came to be regarded as holy or authoritative.
So people ask: When was Daniel canonised? – meaning:
When did Daniel come to be regarded as a scriptural
book, with all the implications just spelled out about universal applicability, hidden meanings, contemporary
relevance, and aptness to be cited with phrases such as,
'As it is written in the book of Daniel'? Its second meaning
is the development of a list (the original meaning of *kanōn*
in Greek) which includes *all* the holy books, and whose
effect is to say that *no other* books have this status. It is
important to see that these are indeed two things, not
one. It is in principle possible to have Scriptures but no
canon, as is certainly the case in many religions. Holy
books simply continue to accumulate until there are more
than any individual could possibly read, and no one feels
the need to impose a cut-off point. Judaism and Christianity could have gone down that road (as Buddhism has
done), but did not in fact do so. It is inconvenient to use
the term 'canonisation' to refer both to recognition of a
book as Scripture and to the decision that it belongs on an
official list while other books do not – and for that reason I
have avoided the term so far. I wanted to keep it for the
fourth development, the inclusion of a book in a definite,
and limited, list.

The point made above about the overlap between our
first three processes – writing, collection, and acceptance
as Scripture – can also be extended to this fourth one.
Clearly it will be true of any given work that it was first
written, then collected into a corpus, then recognised as
Scripture, and only then 'canonised' in the sense of being
officially accepted as part of a limited list. But just as the
other processes overlap chronologically, with some books

having 'arrived' before others had even been written, so
the canonisation of certain books may have happened
very early. So may the *non*-canonisation of others – that
is, their official rejection from the category of Scripture. It
was already clear by the end of the fourth century BC that
nothing could be added to the Pentateuch, that nothing
else could compete with its authority for Jews. And at
that time many other books in the Hebrew Scriptures
had not yet been written at all. Paul gives orders in 2
Thessalonians 2:2 that spurious letters purporting to
come from him are to be ignored, and appends his signature by way of authentication of this letter (3:17). (Some
think 2 Thessalonians is itself spurious, and that this
is an ingenious way of putting it beyond reproach.) And
Tertullian, in the second century AD, refers to lists of 'pro-
hibited' books, suggesting that the Church had already
begun to ban certain texts – although at that time the
contents of the New Testament were by no means fixed.

   The main point to be made, however, about canonisation (in the sense of the official listing of accepted books)
is how little of it actually occurred. Overwhelmingly, in
both Judaism and Christianity, the criterion for using and
revering particular books was the fact (or the belief,
whether or not well-founded) that they always had been
revered. Consequently, as we shall see, it is only at the
margins of the canon that decisions were actually
required in either religion: the great bulk of the biblical
books were simply received from the past and transmitted to the future, with no questions asked.

THE OLD TESTAMENT

That long acceptance was nearly everything in the formation of the Bible is especially clear in the case of the
Hebrew Scriptures. Judaism has displayed little tendency

to legislate about the contents of Scripture, and there is hardly any evidence that there were any disputes about it. There is a passage in the Mishnah (Yadaim 3:5) which says that there were disputes, in the rabbinic academy established at Yavneh after the fall of Jerusalem to the Romans in AD 70, about whether Ecclesiastes and the Song of Songs 'defiled the hands'. This strange idea (perceived as strange at the time – how can a holy book bring defilement?) has been interpreted as implying that some people had doubts about the scriptural status of these two, late and unusual, books. I myself believe that the problem was probably the fact that the divine name, YHWH, does not occur in either book: in which case the dispute was not whether they were scriptural – if they had not been, the problem would not have arisen anyway – but about whether they had to be handled with the care which always attended books containing the Name, as we saw in Chapter 2. Interestingly there is later evidence for questions about whether Esther defiles the hands. Esther also lacks the Name, but was a core part of the Bible for the rabbis, being the primary text read publicly at the feast of Purim. It is inconceivable that anyone tried to decanonise it.

The rabbis did undoubtedly discuss Ecclesiasticus (Sirach), and there are explicit rulings that, though edifying, it is not to be reckoned scriptural. A few doubts are also recorded about Ezekiel, on the basis that it conflicts with the Torah (see above), and about Proverbs, on the ground of internal inconsistency. No other books seem to have been the subject of any rulings, so far as we can tell.

Yet there is surely a great gap in our knowledge here: for this leaves out the question of the longer Greek Old Testament, preserved in Christian manuscripts but certainly the product of Judaism in the Greek-speaking areas, especially Egypt. At some point, rabbinic Judaism must have decided that the shorter, Hebrew Bible was to be preferred over the longer list of the LXX (or Septuagint). And although we distinguish the two lists as 'Hebrew' and 'Greek', it must be remembered that most of the additional books in the LXX canon were originally written in Hebrew. Substantial parts of the Hebrew text of Ecclesiasticus, for example, were discovered in Cairo in 1896, and it is possible to tell from the style of other books that they are translations of a Hebrew original. So it is not simply the question of language that enabled some books to find their way into the Jewish canon while others remained outside.

It used to be thought that the problem could be resolved by saying that the longer and shorter canons represent simply the Scriptures of the Jews of Egypt (Alexandria) and Palestine respectively. The demise of the longer canon in Judaism would then be a consequence of the eventual ascendancy of Palestinian Judaism over the Alexandrian variety. This probably oversimplifies matters, for there was a lot of contact between the two centres of Judaism. A better solution is probably to think that only the Pentateuch was fully canonical – that is, defended against addition or supplantation – by the first century BC, and that all other Jewish books formed a fluid category, from which Jewish communities and writers selected those they liked or, perhaps, those they managed to get copies of. When New Testament writers refer to 'the law and the prophets' as a way of describing the Jewish Bible, 'the law' is fixed but 'the prophets' is still an open-ended list. All the books that are now in the Hebrew Bible were definitely included, but there was a penumbra of works of which some approved, and which no one had yet proscribed. One can imagine this easily in the case of Daniel. The main Hebrew and Aramaic text was a given – authentic, since Daniel had prophesied in the sixth century BC, and so the text had the authority of age. But there were also little additions – the stories of Susanna and Bel and the Dragon, and the hymns sung by the Three Young Men in the fire. Were these genuine or not? We have no records of any discussion about this (on the Christian side, there is a letter by Origen about Susanna, but there is nothing in the Jewish tradition), and probably some thought one thing and some another.

The potential authoritativeness of the Greek canon can be seen, as noted above, in Paul's use of Wisdom. It was also important for Philo of Alexandria, the Jewish writer who was Paul's older contemporary. The Jewish historian Josephus, on the other hand, writing in Greek but from a Palestinian background, does not use what would come to be known as the Apocryphal books – possibly a slight confirmation that the two canons were after all respectively Alexandrian and Palestinian. What is not always noticed is that Josephus' own discussion of the canon, while it reckons with only the books of the present Hebrew Bible, uses as the criterion for inclusion not any decision or ruling of some competent authority, but simply the date of the books. Any book written before the death of Artaxerxes is potentially scriptural; none written after it is. In practice this means that Josephus supports the Hebrew canon (which he knew in Greek!), and hence he can say that there are only 22 sacred books for Jews. But in theory the canon is not closed: a freshly discovered old book would have to be considered a candidate for inclusion. (How Josephus counted the books, and whether they are precisely the same as the present Hebrew books, traditionally counted as 24, remains uncertain.)

The evidence of the New Testament does not help us much. As we have seen, some New Testament writers undoubtedly quote from books which are now in the Apocrypha, Wisdom being the most important. So, on the one hand, it is impossible to argue that the Old Testament canon used by the New Testament Church was absolutely identical to the present Hebrew Scriptures. On the other hand, the use made of (now) non-canonical books is very small by comparison with the massive use of central books such as Genesis, Isaiah or the Psalms. If we are interested in the practical rather than the theoretical position, we shall have to say that for the New Testament the canon is *almost* identical to the Hebrew Bible. The New Testament evidence does not support a doctrinaire assertion that the Apocrypha was non-canonical for these writers, but it does indicate that it was marginal.

By the time of the compilation of the Mishnah, in the second century AD, the Hebrew Bible certainly existed in its present compass: no other book is ever cited there. We still do not know that the Bible had its present shape of Law, Prophets, and Writings – though this is probable. How this came about we do not know.

Once Jews had decided on the shorter Hebrew canon, Christians were bound sooner or later to question whether they should follow suit, or stick to the longer Greek Bible which had been normal for most writers of the first Christian century or so. The bishop and theologian Melito of Sardis (died *c.* AD 190) raised the issue towards the end of the second century, and actually went on a fact-finding tour to Palestine to discover exactly what the limits of the Hebrew canon were. He duly commended it to the Church, which simply continued to use the additional Greek books as though he had never existed.

The only real controversy over the Old Testament canon in the early centuries was between Jerome (*c.* 345–420), the translator of the Bible into Latin, and Augustine of Hippo (354–430). Jerome had settled in Bethlehem, was aided in his work by a number of Jewish advisers, and could hardly fail to realise that the Jews by then gave no place to the apocryphal books at all. He duly proposed that his new Latin Bible, the Vulgate, should follow the shorter Hebrew list. Augustine was strongly opposed to this, arguing that the LXX, and its early Latin version the *Vetus Latina*, had always included the additional books, which Christian leaders and teachers had regularly cited as Scripture. The resolution of the conflict, if it can be called that, was that Jerome translated the extra books, but referred to them as 'apocrypha' (hidden books) or 'ecclesiastical books', by contrast with the canonical books of the Hebrew Scriptures, and no longer treated them as fully scriptural. But since they still appeared in the Latin Bible, most people did not distinguish them from the rest of Scripture. It is particularly interesting that Jerome himself went on using and quoting the deuterocanonical books just as much after his dispute with Augustine as before. Much the same is true of another Christian Father, Athanasius (c. 296–373), who, a generation before Jerome, had similarly declared himself in favour of the shorter canon. His own liking for the apocryphal books, especially for the Wisdom of Solomon, remained just as great after he had so decided. What we see here is a phenomenon to which studies of the biblical canon have often paid too little attention: that people's *theoretical* canon is seldom the same as their *functional* one. Christian writers often use books which they do not regard as canonical; conversely, they accept some books as canonical, but hardly ever use them.

Augustine's acceptance of the whole Greek canon remained the official position of the Western Church until the Reformation. Though the additional books continued to be dubbed apocryphal or deuterocanonical, this made no practical difference – especially as these books were not hived off into a special section, but were mixed in with the Hebrew books of the same type: Wisdom and

Ecclesiasticus next to Proverbs and Ecclesiastes; Tobit and Judith next to Esther; and so on. The Protestant Reformers, however, returned to Jerome's position, and insisted that the Church's Old Testament should contain only the books of the Hebrew canon. However, they achieved this by simply removing the additional books which had come from of the Greek canon, so that the Protestant Old Testament does not follow the order of the Hebrew Bible, but the order of the LXX, only without certain books. It can fairly be said that Protestant Bibles are a hybrid, having the Hebrew books in the Greek order. Paradoxically, the Protestant attempt to restore the primitive and authoritative Bible succeeded in producing a Bible which no Christian had ever known until that moment. Not all Protestants were entirely happy with the change. Anglicans insisted on retaining the apocryphal books, both for private study and for public reading in church (a bold step), Lutherans for private study; but both collected these additional books into an appendix to the Bible, and used the title Apocrypha for them.

THE NEW TESTAMENT

We have already seen that Christians began to collect the writings of the evangelists and letter-writers at a very early date, and soon came to treat them as authoritative and 'scriptural'. For example, at the very end of the first century AD, Clement, Bishop of Rome, in writing to the church at Corinth, quotes from Paul's Corinthian correspondence as though it had binding authority similar to that of the Old Testament Scriptures. The Gospels, similarly, are quoted by Justin Martyr as if they were a Christian equivalent to the Old Testament.

What we do not find, however, are any lists indicating which Christian texts have this special status and which do not. There is general agreement that the first person to make such a list was a heterodox Christian, Marcion, already discussed above in Chapter 3. Marcion's list was very short, consisting of one Gospel – an expurgated, de-Judaised version of Luke – and a few of Paul's letters, arranged so as to begin with Galatians, which is the clearest statement of Paul's idea that Christ has saved his followers from 'the curse of the law' – Marcion took this to mean 'from Judaism'.

It is often claimed that, when he drew up this 'canon', Marcion set a precedent which the Church at large then followed. Instead of holding on to a vaguely defined New Testament, mainstream Christian writers (it is thought) were goaded into listing the books which they, the orthodox, held to be scriptural. But if this is so, no Christian writers of the early centuries seem to have been aware of it. They all unhesitatingly see Marcion's importance as lying in his rejection of the Old Testament, which spurred orthodox writers on to defend the Old Testament and to define its proper place in the Church. No one seems to have thought Marcion's delineation of the New Testament canon to have been at all influential. It is probably preferable to think that Marcion lived at a time when interest in the theoretical boundaries of Christian Scripture was just beginning to arise, and that he simply happens to be our earliest witness to this trend. At all events, whether or not they were spurred on by the need to confute Marcion, Christian writers from the mid second century onwards did begin to take an interest in which 'New Testament' books are genuinely inspired/ apostolic/scriptural, and lists start to appear.

Two classic lists from the fourth century are those of Eusebius and Athanasius. The contents of their lists are very similar, and correspond more or less with our New Testament (Athanasius' does so exactly); but more interesting are the categories into which they classify the various books.

Eusebius distinguishes three categories: books universally acknowledged (in Greek, *homolegoumena*); books whose status is disputed, but which are widely read in the Church (*antilegomena*); and books which should be rejected as spurious (*notha*). The third category includes works such as the *Shepherd* by Hermas, the Epistle of Barnabas, and the Teaching of the Apostles, which were widely revered in the early Church but not reckoned as canonical in any mainstream church in Eusebius' day. The interesting category is the second, books which are said to be disputed. This includes, for Eusebius, James, Jude, 2 Peter, and 2 and 3 John. The rest of what we now know as the New Testament consists of agreed books (category 1). A special case, however, is the book of Revelation, about which doubts were often raised in the Eastern churches – its speculations about the future were widely seen as inflammatory. Eusebius says that this book may belong in category 1 or category 3 – that is, some think of it as universally acknowledged, whereas others think it is spurious. Logically this ought to make it a perfect candidate for category 2, but Eusebius does not seem to see this. It therefore remains, in effect, in a category of its own (not that Eusebius would have felt sure about that, either).

A number of important points arise from this discussion. First, canonicity is generally not a matter of being simply 'in' or 'out': there is a marginal category of books whose status is unclear, not unlike the deuterocanonical books of the Old Testament. Books fall into one of *three* categories, not just of two. If this is true of the official canon, it is even more obviously true where the functional canon is concerned. All Christian writers have books of which they make full and frequent use (category 1), and other books of which they disapprove even if others ascribe authority to them (category 3). But there is nearly always a pen-umbra of books which are either accepted in principle, yet used little, or rejected in principle, yet still used. A good example of the first type is Acts, which Christian writers universally regarded as scriptural, yet which is cited very little in most early Christian writers – certainly far less than its other half, the Gospel according to Luke. The second type can be seen in the *Shepherd of Hermas*, which went on being read in antiquity long after it had been declared uncanonical, and sometimes appears in biblical manuscripts, including the great and prestigious Codex Sinaiticus (mid fourth century AD), divided into sections for public reading in church.

Secondly, though in lists such as that of Eusebius the Church appears to be identifying and defining the books of the New Testament, in practice the great majority were not in any doubt. No one began to take the Gospel of Matthew seriously because Eusebius had listed it! It, and all the other *homolegoumena*, were just that: already agreed by all. It is only at the margins of the canon that a list like this represents a ruling on a controversial topic; and precisely here it does not tell us what we need to know. There is something slightly comic about a solemn declaration that people seem not to be able to agree about the staus of 2 Peter or 3 John – for presumably the readers knew that, and that is precisely why they were reading Eusebius: they hoped that he could tell them the answer to the question. All he does is to state the problem, and leave it unresolved. A very important aspect of the New Testament, as of the Old, was that it had fuzzy edges; all Eusebius does is to identify the exact area of fuzziness.

Thirdly, Eusebius tends to confuse two questions: whether books were orthodox or unorthodox, and whether they were canonical or uncanonical. His *notha*, 'spurious books', are not books that Christians are forbidden to read on the grounds that they are unorthodox or misleading; they are simply books that Christians had, by Eusebius' day, decided were not part of the New Testament. They are orthodox but uncanonical – much as a modern Christian might regard the writings of C. S. Lewis: perfectly orthodox but obviously not part of the Bible. Eusebius then had, in effect, a fourth category, consisting of unorthodox, heretical, thoroughly reprehensible books that no Christian should read, and he instances the Gospel of Peter, a 'worse than spurious' work. When he comes to discuss the book of Revelation, he seems to be changing horses in midstream, and it is hard to tell whether he is addressing the question of its scriptural status or its orthodoxy. If orthodox, it could logically have belonged in category 1 or category 3; if unorthodox it would have had to be assigned to the limbo of heretical works. Yet again, where we need to know the answer to the problem, Eusebius merely tells us that there is a problem.

All this confirms that the recognition of certain books as scriptural was overwhelmingly a natural process, not a matter of ecclesiastical regulation. The core of the New Testament was accepted so early that subsequent rulings do no more than recognize the obvious. And where there was doubt, such rulings all too often allow it to remain.

Thus canonisation, in the sense of making an exclusive list of the books to be received as scriptural, is quite weakly attested in the ancient Church. For the most part, the New Testament books made their own way in the Church, and those which were of doubtful character were seldom either finally accepted or finally rejected by ecclesiastical fiat. A consensus slowly emerged. To this day, even though we now have Bibles in which all the books are printed in the same format and thus look as though they have equal status, most Christians who read the Bible know that this is not really so. If Eusebius was unclear about the standing of 2 Peter and 3 John, so are most modern Christians; and ecclesiastical committees still debate whether it is appropriate to read Revelation in church.

Still, the New Testament as we have received it was endorsed, without addition or deletion, by one authority in the Church of the fourth century AD. The evidence is a letter written by Athanasius to his clergy in AD 367. Note that here the old arrangement, whereby Acts introduces not the Pauline epistles but the Catholic epistles, still survives, but in other respects the list is identical to our own.

> It is not tedious to speak of the [books] of the New Testament. These are the four Gospels, according to Matthew, Mark, Luke, and John. After these, the Acts of the Apostles and Epistles called Catholic, of the seven apostles: of James, one; of Peter, two; of John, three; after these, one of Jude. In addition, there are fourteen epistles of Paul the apostle, written in this order: the first, to the Romans; then, two to the Corinthians; after these, to the Galatians; next, to the Ephesians; then, to the Philippians; then, to the Colossians; after these, two of the Thessalonians; and that to the Hebrews; and again, two to Timothy; one to Titus; and lastly, that to Philemon. And besides, the Revelation of John. These are fountains of salvation, that he who thirsts may be satisfied with the living words they contain. In these alone the teaching of godliness is proclaimed. Let no one add to these; let nothing be taken away from them.

Here is canonisation in the strict, hard sense of the term: the declaration that these books *and only these* are to be regarded as sacred Scripture. Once this point is reached, we can say that the making of the Christian Bible is complete.

Conclusion

In this book we have looked at two processes which are separate, yet which interlock at many points. The first is the process by which the various books that now form the Bible came to be written. The second is the process by which they came to be accepted as Holy Scripture, and distinguished from all other books. Both processes are almost infinitely complex, but certain general tendencies and principles can nevertheless be discerned.

To begin with the writing of the biblical books: we noted that all the cultures which produced the Old and New Testaments were literate cultures, not in the sense that literacy was very widespread, but in that there was a large, élite group of people who were highly literate – as literate as anyone is today – and who produced sophisticated writing for their contemporaries to read. In both Old and New Testament times there were people called, in a technical sense, scribes, and although we have no detailed information about their role, it is clear that they were not merely the ancient equivalent of word-processors, but often produced original and creative writing. Much of the Old Testament comes to us from the hands of such people, and is of a high order of literary excellence.

At the same time, two factors made the situation in ancient times distinctively different from ours. One is the importance attributed to ideas, stories, poems and sayings transmitted orally rather than in writing. Some literate cultures, such as our own, regard oral tradition as less reliable than transmission in writing, but in ancient Israel and in the early Church great store was set by the accuracy of memory, and there are many expressions of the belief that writing is a second-best to a well-trained memory. Early Christians were particularly attached to this point of view, sometimes seeing even the written Gospels as mainly repositories of material which could *remind* the preacher or teacher of the story of Jesus, rather than being a Scripture in its own right – hence the fact that early writers often quote the Gospels inaccurately! Christian preference for the codex rather than the scroll may reflect this idea that the written Gospels were informal, note-like compositions, rather than books in the formal sense. In ancient Israel, too, historical memories probably circulated for many years orally before anyone wrote them down – this would be especially true of the more legendary kinds of material, such as, for example, the stories about Elijah and Elisha.

Secondly, ancient writers had a different idea from us of what constituted original composition. Many of their works are the product of a kind of consortium of writers spread across time, adding to (and sometimes subtracting from) already existing documents, changing these to suit their own particular purposes – producing new editions, cutting documents in half and then developing each half in a new way, combining written material with oral traditions which they happened to know. A book is not the same kind of thing in such a culture as it is for us – an entity with a definite shape, a beginning, a middle, and an end, written in the same style throughout and designed to make a specific point. A modern parallel to the ancient book would be something more like a collection of e-mail messages, combined by the person who received them all and then printed out in a uniform format which concealed their disparate origins.

Nevertheless, over a period of time distinct books did emerge, and acquired names and alleged authors. And

some scriptural books – most obviously the letters of
Paul, but also a few Old Testament books such as Ruth or
Jonah – began life as books even in our sense, as the
writings of one specific person with a message to impart.

The gathering together of separate books into a larger
corpus, and the idea that this corpus had a unique
religious status, was also highly complex. Either the
whole or part of this process tends to be called the canonisation of the Bible, though I have suggested that this
word is better kept for the last stage in the development –
the stage at which it is positively asserted that no other
books than the list being referred to count (or even could
ever count) as Holy Scripture. At any rate, there are
clearly several stages involved.

First, books had to be collected: the books of Moses, for
instance, were gathered together to form the Pentateuch
or Torah; Paul's letters were collected as the Pauline
corpus, and then given wide currency as a coherent collection expressing the same theology throughout, instead
of as individual works, each from a different situation.
Secondly, such collections came to be read in special ways
which do not apply to secular books – allegorically, for
example, or as universally relevant, or as full of hidden
meaning. Finally, there comes the moment where some
competent authority pronounces that the category of
scriptural books is now full, and draws a line under the
collection to turn it into The Holy Bible.

The last of these stages – the one to which I would
unequivocally attach the name canonisation – is less
important than it sounds for either the Old or the New
Testament. There is no record of any authority in
Judaism pronouncing on the exact limits of the Hebrew
Scriptures, only a few stray remarks about this book or
that whose authority was questioned (Ecclesiasticus is in
fact almost the only book we know to have been ruled non-

canonical). And in Christianity, a number of early writers do list the approved books of the New Testament, but for the most part the books listed are entirely obvious (it was not news in the fourth century AD, for example, to be told that Romans was canonical), and where they are not, the list often includes a note confirming that their status is uncertain, rather than a decision about it.

If there is one single point that I should like the reader of this book to take away, it is closely linked to this last observation. The status of the books in our Bibles has only occasionally been controversial. On the fringes of the canon of both Testaments are some books whose status has never been entirely clear in the Church, and in practice (if not in theory) it often remains uncertain today. Where the Old Testament is concerned, the books which Protestants call the Apocrypha have genuinely been the subject of controversy and tension within the Christian Church. But none of them has ever been as important as most of the books in the Old Testament proper for the majority of Christians. Perhaps the (apocryphal) Wisdom of Solomon, a great favourite with early Christian writers, has sometimes been more important than a short and fairly unimportant book, such as the (canonical) prophecy of Nahum. But it would be hard to find a second case of such an upside-down state of affairs. The early Church did, for the most part, regard the Apocrypha as sacred Scripture, but it did not use it much at all. Similarly with the New Testament canon: there were disputes about Hebrews and Revelation, but even those who were keen to include these books in the canon did not use them anything like so much as they used Matthew or Romans.

Thus it is at the margins, not at the centre, that there was controversy. The central core of both Testaments was never controversial in Judaism or in Christianity. The Bible grew by the steady acceptance of certain books as being obviously holy. Often subsequently reasons were discovered (or invented) to support this state of affairs: the date or authorship of the books, or both, were pleaded as reasons for sanctity. But in practice a perception that the books had been used since time immemorial was the real reason. This perception might be a true one – e.g. 1 Thessalonians really is from the earliest period of Christian history; many of the Psalms may well go back to the time of David. Or it may be a false one – e.g. 2 Peter is not by the apostle Peter but by a pseudonymous writer of the very late first century, if not of the second; the book of Deuteronomy is not by Moses but (probably) by a writer or writers from between the seventh and the fifth centuries BC. But whether the perception is true or not, it led to the books being regarded as unassailable long before anyone started to ask, actively, whether this one or that was to be regarded as genuinely canonical. Long usage was (almost) everything. The Bible was not the result of some kind of legislation: it simply grew.

Glossary

allegory A way of interpreting texts in which each surface meaning is taken to refer to some deeper reality. Found in Greek and Hebrew culture, and adopted enthusiastically by Christians.

amanuensis A secretary who takes down a writer's words from dictation, sometimes using shorthand.

apocryphal Protestant designation for the books which are in the Greek Old Testament but not in the Hebrew Scriptures. Protestant Bibles collect them together into a supplement called the Apocrypha.

Aramaic A Semitic language related to Hebrew, which was the lingua franca of the ancient world until the ascendancy of Greek after Alexander the Great. It seems to have been the everyday language of Palestine in the time of Jesus, having ousted Hebrew during the period of Persian domination (sixth to fourth centuries BC). Hebrew and Aramaic are not mutually comprehensible, being about as close as German and Dutch.

ark In a synagogue, the chest holding the scrolls of the Pentateuch. (No connection with Noah's ark, which in Hebrew is a completely different word.)

authenticity The state of affairs when a document is correctly attributed to its true author – thus Romans is authentic if it really was written by Paul, as it claims. In itself, inauthenticity does not necessarily imply inferiority of content.

Book of the Twelve Traditional Jewish name for the books called 'the Minor Prophets' by Christians: Hosea, Joel, Amos, Obadiah, Jonah, Micah, Nahum, Habakkuk, Zephaniah, Haggai, Zechariah, Malachi.

canon The official list of the books accepted as Scripture in a particular Church.

canonisation The inclusion of a given book in a canon; (more loosely) the recognition of a book as having scriptural status.

catholic epistles The letters of James, Peter, John and Jude, taken to be intended for the universal (catholic) Church rather than (as with Paul's letters) for specific churches. Sometimes also called the **general epistles**.

Christology Theories about the nature of Christ and his relationship to God the Father.

codex A book bound between covers, read by turning the pages. Used in antiquity only for notebooks, the form became normal for scriptural books through (unexplained) Christian use.

covenant The special relationship between Israel and its God, taken to involve obligations on both sides.

cuneiform A system of writing used in ancient Mesopotamia, in which signs are incised into stone or clay using a wedge-shaped tool.

deuterocanonical Traditional Roman Catholic name for the semi-canonical works which Protestants call the Apocrypha.

Deuteronomistic History Modern scholarly name for the books Joshua, Judges, Samuel and Kings, which show heavy dependence on the ideas of Deuteronomy. Known in Jewish tradition as the **Former Prophets**.

Diatessaron A harmony of the Gospels made by Tatian in the third century AD, and popular well into the Middle Ages in many languages.

encyclical A letter sent by a Pope to all the churches under his jurisdiction; here used by analogy for the letters of Paul (especially Ephesians) which may have been meant for several different churches.

Enneateuch Early Christian name for the Pentateuch plus the Deuteronomistic History.

epistle Older name for 'letter', still commonly used in biblical studies.

eschatology In Christian theology, teaching about the four last things (death, judgement, heaven, hell); in biblical study, a system of belief about the end-time, when human history will come to its climax.

Ethiopic A general name for the various languages of Ethiopia, all related (but distantly) to Hebrew.

evangelion (or *euangelion*) Greek for 'gospel'.

Exile The catastrophic events of 598 and 587 BC which resulted in many of the ruling class of Judah being exiled to Babylonia, and in which Jerusalem, including its Temple, was destroyed. Hence **pre-exilic** and **post-exilic** as indications of the time before and after the 590s.

gnosticism A system of thought popular in the first few centuries AD which distinguished sharply between flesh and spirit, and believed that the God and Father of Jesus Christ had no contact with the evil, physical world, except to rescue people from it.

Gospel of Thomas A work discovered in Egypt which preserves some sayings of Jesus, and which some scholars think may be authentic. It contains no narrative.

haftarah (plural *haftarot*) The second reading in synagogue liturgy, taken from the prophetic books.

Hexateuch Christian name for the Pentateuch plus Joshua.

Israel The people of God; in the period before 598 BC, the nation-state which controlled Palestine from the time of Saul to the Exile; before 721 BC, sometimes the name of the northern kingdom with its capital at Samaria, by contrast with Judah.

Johannine Deriving from John: hence 'the Johannine literature', meaning the Gospel of John, 1, 2, and 3 John, and Revelation.

Judah The southern of the two Hebrew kingdoms from the reign of David till the Exile; after the Exile, the Persian province which covered much the same area was called Yehud.

LXX The Septuagint (Roman numerals for 70, from the 70 translators who worked on it, according to Jewish legend).

Maccabees Jewish freedom fighters of the second century BC, who opposed the repressive policies of the pagan king Antiochus Epiphanes (or Antiochus IV).

Mishnah An ordered collection of rulings on matters of Torah, assembled in the second century AD by Rabbi Judah the Prince.

Muratorian Fragment A fragmentary list of the canon of the Bible, usually attributed to the second century AD, but nowadays sometimes dated in the fourth.

papyrus A reed, grown mainly in Egypt, from which a substance like paper was made – the main writing material in biblical times.

Pastoral Epistles The letters of Paul to Timothy and Titus, which are almost exclusively about the exercise of ministry in the Church; widely thought to be pseudonymous.

patristic Connected with the Christian writers ('Fathers') of the first five centuries AD.

Pauline Deriving from Paul: hence 'the Pauline letters'.

Pentateuch The five 'books of Moses': Genesis, Exodus, Leviticus, Numbers, Deuteronomy.

Petrine Deriving from Peter; hence 'the Petrine epistles', meaning 1 and 2 Peter.

pseudonymity The practice of attributing a writing to someone other than its true author – sometimes a seer of ancient times (Enoch, Ezra, Daniel), sometimes an apostle (thus probably the Pastoral Epistles).

Q A hypothetical document which may explain the material common to Matthew and Luke but not in Mark (from German *Quelle*, 'source').

Qoheleth The Hebrew name of the book of Ecclesiastes, where it is either the name or the title of the author.

rabbis, rabbinic In general a rabbi is an authorised Jewish teacher with the authority to pronounce on matters of

Torah. More specifically the term is used to refer to the successors of the Pharisees, who codified Jewish law in the Mishnah and Talmud, and whose style of Judaism supplanted the diversity of 'Judaisms' that existed in the New Testament period.

revelation Disclosure by God of matters that cannot be known by ordinary means.

rollers The two rigid bars attached to opposite ends of a scroll, enabling it to be rolled from one hand to the other.

scribe Like 'secretary' in English, a very wide term covering royal officials, administrators and professional writers. Sometimes used in the Gospels for those who taught the Torah, but in the Old Testament it usually implies someone who made a living by writing, not necessarily in the religious sphere.

Septuagint The main Greek translation of the Old Testament, produced primarily in Egypt between about the fourth and first centuries BC.

Synoptic Gospels (sometimes simply **the Synoptics**) The Gospels according to Matthew, Mark and Luke, which tell much the same story and share a common perspective on the life of Jesus, by contrast with John.

Talmud Accumulated rabbinic comment on the Mishnah, compiled from the second to the sixth century AD. There are two Talmuds, the Babylonian and the Palestinian: together they amount to several million words.

Tetrateuch Name sometimes given by scholars to Genesis, Exodus, Leviticus and Numbers – i.e. the Pentateuch without Deuteronomy.

Torah The teaching or instruction by which to live a characteristically Jewish life; sometimes approximately equivalent to 'law'; sometimes used as an alternative name for the Pentateuch (which may also be called the Written Torah, by contrast with the Oral Torah, the accumulated teaching of rabbis and sages).

Biographies

These very brief biographical notes concentrate mainly on the relevance of the person in question to the formation of the Christian Bible.

Athanasius (*c.* 296–373)
Bishop of Alexandria, in Egypt. His Festal Letter of 367 is notable as the first complete listing of the New Testament books which corresponds exactly with our own.

Augustine of Hippo (354–430)
Bishop of Hippo in modern Algeria, prolific preacher and writer. Important for the question of the biblical canon because of his controversy with Jerome about the status of the deuterocanonical books. (Not to be confused with Augustine of Canterbury, who evangelised the south of England.)

Celsus (second century)
A pagan philosopher who attacked Christianity in his work *A True Discourse*, and was in turn attacked by Origen. Their disagreement over how far the New Testament is meant to be allegorised has some importance for the history of the scriptural canon, because allegorisation is often the mark of a holy book.

Clement of Alexandria (*c.* 150–*c.* 215)
A Christian teacher in Alexandria, in Egypt, who wrote extensively on all aspects of the Christian faith. He commented on the Gospels, and is responsible for calling John the 'spiritual' Gospel, implying that its true difference from the Synoptics is in its style of teaching rather than in detailed factual discrepancies.

Clement of Rome (flourished *c.* 96)
Bishop of Rome, who wrote to the Corinthian church in conscious imitation of Paul's correspondence with the same church 40 years or so earlier. Attests the esteem in which 1 Corinthians was held by then.

Eusebius of Caesarea (*c.* 260–*c.* 340)
The first Church historian, who played a critical role in many controversies about details of the Christian faith. Many quotations of early Christian writers have survived only as part of his *Ecclesiastical History*. He records a number of opinions about the origins of the Gospels and other scriptural books.

Irenaeus (*c.* 130–*c.* 200)
Bishop of Lyons but probably a native of Asia Minor (now Turkey). He wrote a detailed attack on gnosticism, a popular religious system of the day, in his work *Adversus haereses* (*Against Heresies*). Importance for the canon of Scripture: he defended the need for the Church to have all four Gospels, and attested to the authority of most other books of the New Testament, while stressing that the Old Testament remained authoritative for Christians.

Jerome (*c.* 345–420)
Christian hermit who translated the entire Bible into Latin, having learnt Hebrew for the purpose (and already knowing Greek). He had a dispute with Augustine about the deutero-canonical books.

Josephus, Flavius (*c.* 37–*c.* 100)
Jewish historian who wrote extensively on the history of the Jews in his own time (*The Jewish War*), and also in biblical times (*The Jewish Antiquities*). In his work *Against Apion*, he defended Judaism as superior to Greek culture, and in the process discussed the number and nature of the scriptural books accepted by the Jews.

Justin Martyr (*c.* 100–*c.* 165)
A native of Palestine, who taught in Ephesus and Rome, where he was martyred. His *Dialogue with Trypho* is a detailed attempt to persuade a Jewish rabbi that the Old Testament Scriptures point to Jesus Christ. He is one of the first to attest to the use of the Gospels in Christian worship, but shows no knowledge of John, which may mean that he did not know this Gospel (other explanations are possible).

Marcion (died *c.* 160)
Developed a heterodox form of Christianity while teaching in Rome, became the subject of powerful attacks from Tertullian, Clement of Alexandria and Origen. Produced a 'canonical' list of the New Testament books, which he limited to Luke and certain Pauline epistles, all expurgated to remove references to the Old Testament, which he rejected. Christian allegiance to the Old Testament probably owes much to the perceived need to combat his system. Some think that his New Testament became the model for the later, orthodox canon of 27 books.

Melito (died *c.* 190)
Bishop of Sardis, who visited Palestine to see the holy places and also to compare Christian Scripture with the books canonical among the Jews. This resulted in a recommendation to discard the deuterocanonical books, but this idea went unheeded.

Origen (*c.* 185–*c.* 254)
Probably the most outstanding scholar in the early Church, who taught in Alexandria, and wrote commentaries on many biblical books as well as philosophical and theological works. He collated manuscripts of biblical texts, in Greek and also in Hebrew. His writings show that he accepted more or less the New Testament as we now have it, and the Old Testament in its longer Greek form.

Philo (*c.* 20 BC–*c.* AD 50)
A Jewish teacher at Alexandria who produced voluminous commentaries on the Pentateuch, marked by a strongly allegorising tendency.

Tatian (flourished *c.* 160)
Came from Assyria and returned to the east after studying at Rome with Justin Martyr. He compiled a 'harmony' of the Gospels, reconciling the discrepancies so as to produce a single, consistent narrative, called the *Diatessaron*, which continued to be used in Syria till the fifth century. In various Western languages it survived into the Middle Ages as an acceptable 'Life of Jesus'.

Tertullian (*c.* 160–*c.* 225)
A native of Carthage in north Africa, probably a lawyer, who converted to Christianity around 197 and began to produce controversial works defending the Christian faith against what he regarded as heresies – though he himself ended his life as a Montanist, a member of a charismatic and apocalyptic sect. His attack on Marcion (*Against Marcion*) provides most of what we know about Marcionism, and documents Marcion's minimalism in accepting only some of the books of the New Testament and none of the Old.

LaVergne, TN USA
05 August 2010
192188LV00001B/1/P